Imagination and Arts-Ba[ ]
Practices for Integration
in Research

Imagination and Arts-Based Practices for Integration in Research explores the philosophical assumptions, defining concepts, and methodological issues related to the introduction of intentional imaginative mental processes and arts-based practices into some or all phases of investigation, and data integration of particular research approaches.

Although typically central to mixed, multi-method, and arts-based research, the practice of integrating diverse forms of data might be applied to other research traditions. The integration of data diversity represents a deviation from traditional scientific thinking demanding a dramatic paradigm shift inclusive of multi-dimensional, nondiscursive, aesthetic, rhizomatic, and imaginative mental processes. In this book, imaginative mental processes and arts-based practices are described and illustrated as approaches to investigating, revealing, and understanding the elusive yet essential meanings hidden in the crevices, shadows, and liminal spaces in between diverse data sets leading to integration, illumination, and synthesis.

The book will appeal to arts-based, mixed methods, and adventurous researchers. It walks the reader through the revisionist philosophical assumptions and offers aligned methodological suggestions to the induction of imaginative mental processes and arts-based practices into research.

Nancy Gerber is an art psychotherapist, educator, and scholar. Through her years of clinical practice, teaching, and research, she has developed an interest in creating ways to capture and study the complexities and dimensions of the human condition through research methods that include and synthesize imaginative processes and arts-based practices.

Developing Traditions in Qualitative Inquiry
Series Editors: Jasmine Brooke Ulmer and James Salvo
Wayne State University

The Developing Traditions in Qualitative Inquiry series invites scholars to share novel and innovative work in accessible ways, ways such that others might discover their own paths, too. In acknowledging who and what have respectively influenced our work along the way, this series encourages thoughtful engagements with approaches to inquiry – ones that are situated within ongoing scholarly conversations. Neither stuck in tradition nor unaware of it, volumes make new scholarly contributions to qualitative inquiry that attend to what's shared across disciplines and methodological approaches. By design, qualitative inquiry is a tradition of innovation in and of itself, one aimed at the target of justice.

From multiple perspectives and positionalities, concise volumes in this series (20,000 to 50,000 words) strengthen and grow the qualitative community by developing inquiry traditions as they should be developed: inclusively, diversely, and together.

For more information about the series or proposal guidelines, please write the Series Editors at jasmine.ulmer@wayne.edu and salvo@wayne.edu.

Other volumes in this series include:

Imagination and Arts-Based Practices for Integration in Research
Nancy Gerber

Transnational Black Feminism and Qualitative Research
Black Women, Racialization and Migration
Tanja J. Burkhard

Shared and Collaborative Practice in Qualitative Inquiry
Tiny Revolutions
Jasmine Brooke Ulmer

For a full list of titles in this series, please visit www.routledge.com/Developing-Traditions-in-Qualitative-Inquiry/book-series/DTQI

Imagination and Arts-Based Practices for Integration in Research

Nancy Gerber

Routledge
Taylor & Francis Group

LONDON AND NEW YORK

First published 2022
by Routledge
4 Park Square, Milton Park, Abingdon, Oxon OX14 4RN

and by Routledge
605 Third Avenue, New York, NY 10158

Routledge is an imprint of the Taylor & Francis Group, an informa business

© 2022 Nancy Gerber

British Library Cataloguing-in-Publication Data
A catalogue record for this book is available from the British Library

Library of Congress Cataloging-in-Publication Data
A catalog record for this book has been requested

ISBN: 978-1-032-19640-4 (hbk)
ISBN: 978-1-032-19642-8 (pbk)
ISBN: 978-1-003-26018-9 (ebk)

DOI: 10.4324/9781003260189

Typeset in Times New Roman
by Apex CoVantage, LLC

Contents

Tables

Acknowledgments

For so many years this little book has been forming and living in my mind and soul. Its conception, growth, and eventual birth is the result of the convergence of so many interactions with amazing and creative thinkers who inspired me, artists who sparked my imagination, friends who encouraged me, students who challenged me, and colleagues who shared ideas. It also is the conflagration of infinite opportunities from conference presentations, hallway coffee consultations, co-created dreams and resultant manuscripts, impassioned classroom dialogues, and dynamic reveries. Paralleling the imaginative process, the development of this book has been an emergent and magical journey that I had not planned and did not even know had begun. It follows the imaginative processes I describe in the book – unconscious initial and embryonic notions, artifactual formations, artistic reflections, conscious dialogues and assemblages, and the final synthesis. Such a journey is conceived in the unconscious; therefore, during its conception there were so many people and events, peripherally and centrally, who were influential in that conception. I cannot possibly recall or acknowledge everyone who contributed to the inspiration for and ultimate creation of this book.

I would like to acknowledge my wonderful colleagues in the Arts-Based Research Global Consortium for their collaborations and inspiration as we embarked on a parallel imaginative research journey that has contributed so much to the conceptualization of this book: Jacelyn Biondo, Karin Hannes, Richard Siegesmund, Madeline Centracchio, Marco Gemignani, Lucia Carriera, and Elisabetta Biffi. These acknowledgments would also be incomplete without mentioning and thanking some of my chief cheerleaders, muses, and encouragers such as Barbara Fitzgerald, David Gussak, Jacelyn Biondo, Juliet King, Elizabeth Templeton, Theresa Van Lith, Amber Ward, Sally Pearne, Dafna Moriya, Victoria Scotti, and Gioia Chilton. My sincere apologies if I have overlooked anyone but I suppose anyone who has touched my life has had a little part in the book's inception and creation and for that I am eternally grateful.

So, although I cannot thank everyone by name, there are a few people who were instrumental in the more pragmatic, intentional, and recent phases of creating this book. First, many thanks and loving gratitude to Hannah Shakespeare, editor and encourager extraordinaire, who has tagged along with me over many years, patiently cultivating promising ideas for books and ultimately arriving at this one. Hannah, you are a treasure. Also, to members of the mixed methods research (MMR) community, I would like to thank them for being so welcoming, open to changing the research discourse, and opening doors to creativity and innovation in research. To John Creswell, Tessa Muncey, Donna Mertens, Kathy Collins, Caryn West, Burke Johnson, and so many more, much appreciation and gratitude for pioneering new and imaginative research pathways. I would also like to thank John Hitchcock and Tony Onwuegbuzie, also from the MMR community, who initially asked me to write a chapter on integration using arts-based approaches, for their book. For a number of reasons that chapter did not happen, but then fortuitously I had the opportunity to turn it into this little book. I would also like to acknowledge my brilliant and sometimes creative writing partner Mandy Archibald, who initiated our explorations of the integration of the arts in mixed methods research. Our many conversations, presentations, and adventures in writing have indeed contributed to this book. Much gratitude and appreciation to James Salvo, who invited me to present on a panel about Art as Resistance which really gave me an opportunity to debut this idea about exploring imagination and research. As a result of that panel, James and Norm Denzin invited me to write a chapter which became my first written piece, from the panel, entitled "Saving Our Soul: Radical Imagination as Activism". That chapter, the precursor for this book, would not have been published without Chris Myers, President and Publisher Myers Education Press. I want to express my deep appreciation for and sincere gratitude to Chris Myers for supporting my use of the essential aspects of that chapter for inclusion in this book. Many thanks to James Salvo and Jasmine Ulmer for inviting me to publish in the innovative book series you have created. I am honored to be sitting among such imaginative thinkers and ideas.

Finally, I would like to extend my heartfelt thanks and infinite gratitude to the students, past and present, who have taught me more than they know! Their passion, commitment, curiosity, and creativity have been a constant life force for me. You know who you are! I am eternally grateful that you touched my life. This book is for you.

Preface

"Imagination is more important than knowledge. For knowledge is limited, whereas imagination embraces the entire world, stimulating progress, giving birth to evolution".
– Albert Einstein, What Life Means to Einstein (1929)

Recently, I was asked to write about the use of the arts in research as an approach to integration in mixed methods research. When thinking about how I would conceptualize and articulate such approaches, I engaged in a spontaneous email communication with some colleagues about existing and emergent perspectives on integration. From this conversation, I was referred to an article referencing Bayesian statistics as one of these perspectives. Statistics is not my greatest strength, so because of my marginal understanding of statistics, the only way I could read the article was by entering into a sort of reverie where visualization and imaginative internal dialogue took me beyond the statistical specifics and into a realm where I thought I could grasp the statistical story or the overall concepts of the article and a resultant conversation. This process opened new insights for revisionist philosophical assumptions, conceptualization strategies, knowledge generation approaches, integration strategies, and interpretational lenses by implementing intentional imaginative mental processes and arts-based practices in mixed and multi-methods research (Gerber, 2020, p. 101). Here is a peek into that email conversation and thought process that inspired this little book on imagination in research.

Memo Insert
July 27, 2018
Dear John,

So here is how my brain works . . . as I was reading your article and email, I started to think in images and pictures. I don't know if this will make sense to you, but I think of images, sensory, and embodied responses as data related to the statistical, the textual or descriptive data. It is almost a type of reverie in which the images or the imagination emerge and tap into pre-verbal, pre-logical, nondiscursive mental data that to me represent the ultimate integration – filling in the interstitial spaces between the qualitative and quantitative data, the conscious and unconscious, the seen and unseen, the known and unknown. . . . My grasp of sophisticated statistical concepts, as I mentioned, is regrettably limited, but in reading your article and your email, I have a notion that these types of visualizations, arts-based and embodied responses to data, interpretation, and integration might have some intriguing intersections that expand the meaning of the more traditional data types and methods. (N. Gerber, personal communication, July 27, 2018; Gerber, 2020, p. 101)

Reference

Gerber, N. (2020). *Saving our soul: Imagination as social activism.* In New Directions in Theorizing Qualitative Inquiry. Myers Education Press.

1 Introduction

Overview

As introduced through the prologue, this book explores the philosophical assumptions, defining concepts, and methodological issues related to the introduction of intentional imaginative mental processes, related pre-verbal data, and arts-based practices into all or some phases of investigation and data integration of particular research approaches. More specifically, the book was inspired by emerging questions and enduring challenges about approaches to the integration and interpretation of diverse and dialectical forms of data that are collected, revealed and used in the research process. Perhaps most relevant to mixed and multi-method research, wherein the integration of concurrent or sequential qualitative and quantitative data is critical to the methodology, integrative processes have both eluded and inspired researchers because integration of diverse forms of data represents a deviation and onto-epistemic shift from more traditional ways of thinking. This paradigmatic shift requires a dramatic and conceptual change from singular scientific linear thinking to inclusive multi-dimensional, rhizomatic, imaginative, and creative mental processes. Imaginative and creative thought has often been considered off-limits or taboo within the dominant research paradigms and hegemonies which prioritize objectivity, linearity, measure, and generalizability as a singular path to truth. From this perspective, the sensory, kinetic, embodied, and emotional ways of experiencing and knowing generated from imaginative and creative processes are considered extraneous, frivolous, and superfluous. However, contemporary and innovative thinkers advocating for the expansion of research philosophy, theory, and methodology in pursuit of a more comprehensive and nuanced truth are revisiting the intentional inclusion of imaginative thought as an inherent and requisite part of research. One of these thinkers is Abbas Tashakkori (personal communication, June, 2007), a pioneer in

DOI: 10.4324/9781003260189-1

mixed methods research. In a keynote at a mixed methods research conference, Tashakkori challenged researchers to be creative inventing new ways to re-conceptualize and use the mixing of methods to expand the scope, possibilities, and meaning of research.

As someone for whom imagination and creativity are essential for my profession and my life, I decided to examine possible intersections between imaginative mental processes, arts-based practices, and integration within multiple research approaches. I intentionally and playfully began to investigate the intersections of imagination, visualization, storying, and arts-based constructions with more typical statistical, textual, and descriptive data for purposes of enhancing insight, understanding, and integration. Intentional playfulness is not a term or process normally associated with research, but perhaps, in varying degrees, improvisational and strategic playfulness might shake up and shake out additional insights hiding in the liminal spaces in big and diverse data shadows. To that end, although originally conceived for consideration in mixed methods research, these theories and practices can conceivably be applied to multiple forms of research in pursuit of more holistic, robust, and nuanced results.

Therefore, this small missive aims to introduce and more fully explore the philosophical assumptions and defining concepts related to the integration of intentional imaginational mental processes and related arts-based practices into all or some phases of investigation and data integration in research. The structure of the book includes this first chapter which serves to present briefly, albeit comprehensively, the major concepts and constructs of the book. These major concepts include a brief definition of imagination, philosophical perspectives related to imaginative mental processes, and conceptual frameworks and practices for integrating imagination in research.

In the subsequent chapters, the concepts introduced in this overview will be elaborated and amplified. First, we visit the current sociopolitical context which requires scholars and researchers to consider the necessity to disrupt obstructive embedded ways of thinking facilitating the acquisition of new knowledge. Therefore, in this book, imaginative mental processes and aesthetic knowledge are invoked as meta perspectives to critically and creatively examine, disrupt, and deconstruct the typical tacitly accepted dominant modes of thought and research (Deleuze & Guattari, 1987; Edwards et al., 2017; Gerber, 2020; Gerber & Myers-Coffman, 2018; Haiven & Khasnabish, 2014; Klooger, 2009; Montuori, 2011; Sardar, 2009). Second, we will take a deeper dive into how the onto-epistemology of imagination relative to its dialectic aesthetic intersubjective nature intersects with and contributes to the understanding of individual, collective, and social assumptions, levels of consciousness, behavior, and research traditions (Castoriadis, 1998; Chilton et al., 2015; Gerber, 2020; Gerber et al., 2020; Haiven & Khasnabish, 2014).

Next, aligned with these contextual, philosophical, and theoretical explorations is the introduction of more intentional methodological approaches for engagement in imaginative processes and arts-based practices in research leading to integrative strategies and final syntheses (Archibald & Gerber, 2018; Gerber & Myers-Coffman, 2018: Scotti & Gerber, 2017). Requisite to the presentation of these new perspectives and practices is a discussion of the competencies and ethical responsibilities of researchers employing these approaches. This discussion reinforces the importance and the inclusion of collaborators with diverse topical, disciplinary, and methodological expertise – the statistician, the narrator, the psychotherapist, and the artist. Finally, pragmatic approaches to including imagination mental processes and arts-based practices at all phases of research are presented with particular emphasis on the comparison, contrast, and merger of diverse forms of data leading to integration, illumination, and synthesis.

On a final note, the writing style of the book at times reflects and parallels the imaginative mental processes employed in the research mode being described. You may find that the text weaves back and forth between philosophy and method, logic and reverie, linearity and meandering with the hope of accompanying the reader on an experience of the imaginative research journey. As described by Deleuze and Guattari (1987), this book is more of an assemblage of multiple dynamic "lines of flight" (p. 3) which may not follow the typical logic or construction of some scientific books but rather follows a creative format parallel to the reverized thinking and imaginative integrative research perspectives and processes proposed in the book.

Brief introduction to imagination

We begin by briefly exploring origins and conceptualizations of imagination that contribute to understanding the philosophical underpinnings of its onto-epistemology and ultimately its implications for research. The terms image and imagination originate from the Latin *imago* relating to artifactual visual perceptions. Visual perceptions are created from the dynamic interaction between segregate or aggregate external environmental and internal mental stimuli (Image, 2020). From the psychoanalytic perspective, which is my predominant worldview, the complex nature of mental imagery was described by Freud (1899/2017) as comprising multiple sources of stimuli which contribute to the construction of dream imagery, often the source of our imaginary world. He categorized these stimuli as originating from four interactive perceptual, sensory, somatic, and emotional sources: external objective sensory stimuli, external subjective sensory stimuli, internal organic somatic stimuli, and psychic stimuli. Although from a dominant paradigmatic perspective some define image binarily, originating from either external or internal stimuli, other worldviews, like those of Freud and Jung (1968), contend that our perceptions of the world are dialectic and dynamic constructions of the interactions between what we see, embody, and/or experience viscerally around us. These constructions form multidimensional snapshots that capture a holistic experience resulting in the creation of the representative symbolic mental imagery in daydreams and dreams essential for imagination. Contrary to the dominant paradigmatic view of imagination as limited to a logical cognitive process of reconfiguring ideas or problem-solving, more pluralistic lenses link imagination to noetic processes of "direct knowing or inner wisdom based on experience or subjective understanding" connecting us to the soul (Swan-Foster, 2018, p. 132). The pluralistic perspective allows us to conceptualize imagination as emanating from multiple intrapsychic and intersubjective sources resulting in the generation of dynamic, multifaceted, aesthetic, and rhizomatic, rather than linear dichotomous, ways of knowing. The multiple sources of imagination, its dialectic aesthetic epistemic, and its pluralistic ontology reflect the ideata and wisdom residing in the individual and collective unconscious which would otherwise be inaccessible. From this view, we can regard imagination as the "active and engaged process of capturing previously unknown images from the unconscious" that manifest through the senses revealing what was formerly invisible (Swan-Foster, 2018, p. 115). Additionally, Symington (1996) suggests that the "[i]nternal picture making, pattern making", of imagination, initiated and nurtured through interpersonal stimuli, helps us to make sense of seemingly disconnected sensory experiences. Without imagination these patterns are experienced as chaos (Symington, 1996, p. 38). In the field of psychotherapy, imagination "is [considered] the psychotherapist's instrument of understanding" (Symington, 1996, p. 35). Human beings make contact with one another through imagination. The "deepest contact between one human being and another occurs through shared fantasy life in the unconscious" (Symington, 1996, p. 35). Of note in this brief overview is the consistent theme of dialectic dynamism between multiple types and sources of stimuli as an emerging imaginative onto-epistemology and its relevance to retrieving and constructing often overlooked or dismissed artifactual and co-created dimensions of knowledge in life and ultimately research (Gerber, 2020).

These defining onto-epistemic features of imagination allow us to consider the co-existence, inclusion, and contributions of previously dismissed invisible aesthetic knowledge – sensory, embodied, and emotional experience – hiding in-between the data spaces and potentially illuminating dimensions of the research phenomena. It follows that these defining features of imaginational mental processes and the resultant imagery include concepts aligned with the philosophy and practice of mixed and multi-method research. In these research approaches, in particular, we collect and imagine relationships between diverse forms of data or stimuli from multiple realities, sources, people, and perspectives in order to construct a holistic picture of the phenomenon under investigation (Gerber, 2020). The dimension of imagination allows us to consider the inclusion of the previously dismissed invisible and artifactual sensory, embodied, and emotional data which further illuminate the depth of and insight into the individual and intersubjective human discourse.

Philosophical perspectives

The onto-epistemic of imagination and related arts-based research practices provides a philosophy and correlate methodologies for integrating pluralistic realities and eclectic ways of knowing essential to mixed methods, multi-method, arts-based, and other forms of research. Emergent from multiple convergent philosophical traditions in psychoanalysis, the humanities, the arts, and anthropology, aligned with more radical critical, interpretivist, and feminist theories, imaginative perspectives and processes and their correlate arts-based practices can form unlikely but progressive partnerships with seemingly incompatible traditional research approaches. With these partnerships come various philosophical and methodological benefits and challenges inherent in introducing imagination processes and arts-based practices into research.

The benefits include serving as both a meta-perspective and a concomitant micro-process. The meta-perspective addresses imagination as a socially engaged activist philosophy at the sociopolitical level, while the micro-processes address the aligned research strategies, actions, and innovative investigative practices used in the conceptualization of research ideas and designs; the generation, analysis, and assemblage of data; and the integration, interpretation, and representation of multi-dimensional knowledge.

As a meta-perspective, imagination can act to disrupt the complacency of the usual which can become stagnant restricting access to innovation and new knowledge. Furthermore, imagination enhances the depth of exploration intensifying the insight into unconscious intersubjective perception, motivation, and behavior; captures multiple voices, celebrates co-existence of difference while leveling the power dynamics of oppression; enriches the understanding of and integration between diverse forms of knowing and ways of being; and increases the evocative impact and disseminative reach of research about the human condition. The benefits are accompanied by challenges which include the radical paradigmatic shifts in philosophical and theoretical perspectives from the dominant worldview that are necessary to understand, embrace, and authenticate imaginative thought and arts-based research approaches. To embrace imaginative perspectives and arts-based methods requires a capacity to tolerate the unknown, trust the creative process, engage in emergent rather than predictive methods, value imaginative knowledge, and equivalate the impact of imaginative and arts-based investigative perspectives with other dominant traditions (Abdullah, 2016; Archibald & Gerber, 2018; Camargo-Borges, 2017; Edwards, Arfaoui, McLaren, & McKeever, 2017; Gerber, 2020; Haiven & Khasnabish, 2014; Montuori, 2011).

Central to these paradigmatic challenges has been the marginalization and dismissal by the dominant research traditions of the imaginative onto-epistemic (Klooger, 2009). Although this dismissive position is tacitly accepted and unquestioned in the scientific community, it is in conflict with the assertion by social scientists, psychoanalysts, and philosophers that imagination is perhaps equal to or more important than science for sustaining life (Haiven & Khasnabish, 2014; Klooger, 2009; Montuori, 2009; Sardar, 2009; Symington, 1996; Urribarri, 2002). For instance, Klooger (2009) posits that "Human life is a creation of psyche and society" (p. 5). And furthermore, the dynamic interaction between psyche and society creates and initiates a necessary dialectical dialogue causing disruptive tensions that require and compel the multi-dimensional thinking of imagination to conceptualize solutions and innovative contributions beyond the usual or familiar (Klooger, 2009). The current social and geo-political climate is challenging implicit assumptions and embedded ideologies, de-stabilizing long-held foundational structures, belief systems, and worldviews. As prophetically described by Sardar (2009), we live in postnormal times "where old orthodoxies are dying, new ones have not yet emerged, and nothing really makes sense" (p. 435). As we experience these dramatic postnormal shifts in the basic ideologies of contemporary culture, the urgency for a collective and concerted effort to re-imagine human-made societal constructs and values becomes increasingly more critical to our physical, psychological, and social survival (Haiven & Khasnabish, 2014; Montuori, 2011; Sardar, 2009). According to Sardar (2009), imagination

> is the main tool, indeed I would suggest the only tool, which takes us from simple reasoned analysis to higher synthesis. While imagination is intangible, it creates and shapes our reality; while a mental tool, it affects our behaviour and expectations.
>
> (p. 443)

In this context, imagination is being centralized by some social scientists as a process required to navigate through these critical ideological and structural shifts. Castoriadis (as cited in Klooger, 2009) called this collective re-imagining "radical imagination". According to Haiven and Khasnabish

(2014), radical imagination "is the ability to imagine the world, life and social institutions not as they are but as they might otherwise be. It is the courage and the intelligence to recognize that the world can and should be changed" (p. 3). Haiven and Khasnabish (2014) argue that radical imagination not only is required for social movements but also is simultaneously a form of socially engaged research requiring the collaborative efforts between the social activists and critically reflexive researchers.

In a radically imaginative movement, the deconstruction and re-imagining of dominant and typical ways of thinking demand the introduction of a creative rather than critical ontology. Disrupting the usual hierarchical, binary perspectives and rejecting familiar complacent practices invoke radically imaginative, organically rhizomatic thought and innovative methods (Deleuze & Guattari, 1987; Edwards et al., 2017; Haiven & Khasnabish, 2014). Progressive worldviews such as (a) "post-structuralism, postmodernism, liquid modernity" (Camargo-Borges, 2018, p. 90); (b) post-qualitative "immanent ontology and transcendental empiricism" of the "'not-yet' . . . that is everywhere but indeterminate, not yet created, not yet individuated and organized into the definite – immanent" (St. Pierre, 2019, p. 4); and (c) the dialectical stance (Greene, 2007) or dialectical pluralistic (Johnson, 2015) perspectives of difference and possibility provide new lenses and theories to guide this re-imagining process. Summoning these more radical worldviews facilitates the imaginative thinking necessary to revolutionize our onto-epistemology freeing us from the hegemony of one philosophical or theoretical approach (Camargo-Borges, 2018, p. 91).

An onto-epistemological revolution is not new but recently re-emerged in the 20th century. Camargo-Borges (2018) highlights this movement during which "a transformation takes place in the concept of knowledge production and what is taken as truth, objectivity, and validity. The epistemological approach here is experiential, propositional, and co-created" (p. 90). The infusion of imaginative, dialectic, aesthetic epistemologies, and pluralistic intersubjective ontological perspectives into research allows for the hierarchical repositioning of experiential, propositional, and co-created ways of knowing and being. Such repositioning shifts the sociopolitical discourse and research focus to embrace multiple co-existing perspectives, include marginalized and multi-voice dialogues, and acknowledge the invisible unconscious perceptions underlying our individual and collective motivation and behavior (Chilton et al., 2015; Camargo-Borges, 2018; Edwards et al., 2017; Eisner, 2008; Greene, 2007; Johnson, 2015; Klooger, 2009; Sardar, 2009). Imagination provides the requisite mental processes and visionary lens to accommodate the "complexities, chaos, and contradictions" (Sardar, 2009, p. 436) of radical change while functioning to embrace the tensions of paradoxical ideas, re-envision perplexing and multiple realities, and conceptualize approaches to radical social re-constructions (Camargo-Borges, 2018; Montuori, 2011; Sardar, 2009). As eloquently described by Haiven and Khasnabish (2014):

> We understand the imagination as our capacity to think about those things we do not or cannot directly experience but it is also the filter or the frame through which we interpret our own experiences . . . empathize with others, the way we gain some sense of the forces that impact our lives, and the way we project ourselves into the future and gain inspiration and direction from the past.
>
> (p. 4)

Therefore, as a meta-perspective, imagination and creativity are considered essential to conceptualizing, tolerating, embracing, and managing paradoxical postnormal dialogues and ideologies while positing a method for reconstructing new discourses and perspectives.

As a micro-process, imagination in research methodology can mirror the dramatically shifting ideologies of the sociopolitical landscape in the conceptualization and design of research projects to systematically study and creatively activate these changes. As asserted by Haiven and Khasnabish (2014), "unlike many, we take seriously the question of the researcher's responsibility not merely to 'observe' and report on the radical imagination but to awaken, enliven and 'convoke' it" (p. 2). Therefore, imagination applies not only to the re-imagining of these sociopolitical meta-structures but also to the creative investigative methods that can address, understand, and initiate change. The imaginative onto-epistemic and the imaginative process opens the investigation to those phenomena and data beyond the obvious in order to dig deep into and understand the workings of the collective human mind, motivation, and experience. To that end, imaginative investigational perspectives and methods are inclusive of dialectical and meandering dialogues between almost-formed internal perceptions and empirical external data; conscious logical thought and unconscious sensory-embodied notions; the researcher and researched; and descriptive visual and statistical or measured numerical data. Additionally, such dynamic dialogues occur in an intersubjective context contributing to the generation of aesthetic interrelational symbol formation, diverse data assemblages, and collective meaning assignment. This dialogical process allows us to imagine the participants, the phenomena, and the data at sensory and embodied levels which, in combination with empirical data, illuminate new formative concepts, raise new questions, re-configure, and construct new social narratives and research directions (Abdullah, 2016; Camargo-Borges, 2018; Chilton et al., 2015; Gemignani, 2011; Haiven & Khasnabish, 2014; Klooger,

2009; Montuori, 2011; Springgay et al., 2008). Summarily, a deeply iterative, creative, and reflective investigative process, imagination embraces the
ambiguity and tension between multiple realities, eclectic and diverse types
of data, and intra- and intersubjective dialectical dialogues to reveal new
dimensions of knowledge beyond the tangible, visible, obvious, and logical into the realm of the unknown or soon-to-be-known (Abdullah, 2016;
Archibald & Gerber, 2018; Camargo-Borges, 2018; Haiven & Khasnabish,
2014; Kapitan, 2010; Montuori, 2011; St. Pierre, 2019).

Conceptual and practical frameworks for imagination and the arts in research

Imagination provides the mindset and mental processes that drive active
research practices. The research practices allow for the emergence, con-
cretization, evaluation, and revelation of imaginative ideas. This is specifically relevant to arts-based forms of inquiry. The arts are particularly
suitable to serve as the visible correlate to imagination since they share the
same epistemic. Imaginative mental processes are precursory and critical
to the understanding and implementation of authentic arts-based research
practices and consequently relevant to understanding the inclusion of
imagination and the arts in multiple forms of research. A discussion of the
multiple perspectives, definitions, and arts-based practices requires further
consideration to clarify the various ways in which the arts are integrated
into research. Arts-based research (ABR) is used as both an umbrella term
inclusive of a continuum of approaches and a philosophical perspective
and specific methodological practices. Along the continuum of approaches,
varying defining characteristics have been proffered to distinguish between
the arts-based research variants. Three categories that highlight the distinctions between the various perspectives and applications of the arts in
research along the continuum are *arts-related, arts-informed, and arts-
based research practice (ABR)* (Gerber et al., 2020). These categories exist
on an interactive continuum rather than a hierarchy, distinguished by the
degree to which the imaginative/arts-based onto-epistemology is centralized, the degree of engagement in the arts by researchers and participants,
and the role of the researcher. For example, the onto-epistemology will
determine the type and degree of arts-based engagement – the arts may
be included as illustrative exemplars, amplifiers of participant generated
qualitative data, or the primary mode of investigation, interpretation, representation, and dissemination. Relative to those decisions are the role and
level of arts-based activity of the researcher in either the strategic selec-
tor of arts-based exemplars, elicitor of participant arts-based responses, or
generator of arts-based data and analysis.

Arts related research may be defined as using pre-existing illustrative examples, such as photographs, literary or dramatic clips, audio recordings, and so on from the arts to complement or amplify particular qualitative and/ or quantitative data. The researcher collects traditional qualitative and/or quantitative data but does not generate arts-based data from participants nor does the researcher participate in arts-based responses (Gerber et al., 2020). *Arts-informed* research is "a mode and form of qualitative research that is influenced by, but not based in the arts" (Cole & Knowles, 2008, p. 59). Arts-informed research centralizes the art process in one or more phases of the research but is reliant mostly upon participant-generated arts-based data to amplify existing qualitative data. In this tradition, some researchers may include strategically placed arts-based responses either during particular phases of the research or as a final presentation such as an installation. *ABR*, as an arts-based practice, is defined as a "systematic use of the artistic process . . . as a primary way of understanding and examining experience" (McNiff, 2008, p. 29). ABR practice centralizes the arts-based inquiry practice and emphasizes the role of the participant/researcher/artist as the generator of the arts-based data in response to the research questions and phenomena. In this role, the researcher uses iterative, data-driven, and in-depth arts-based responses throughout all investigative, analytic, interpretative, and representational phases of research process to illuminate the research phenomena (Archibald & Gerber, 2018; Barone & Eisner, 2012; Eisner, 2008; Gerber & Myers-Coffman, 2018; Leavy, 2020; McNiff, 2008; Springgay et al., 2008).

Summarily, it might be helpful to review these concepts, the degrees of arts-based involvement, and categorical distinctions between approaches on the philosophical and methodological continuum here in more detail (also see Table 1.1): (a) the degree to which the imaginative artistic process is onto-epistemologically and methodologically centralized; (b) the use of arts processes to illustrate and illuminate descriptive data; (c) the positioning and primacy of the imaginative process and artistic inquiry in the generation, interpretation, and representation of the data; (d) the strategic decisions and implementation of multiple or singular arts genre(s) in the phases of research; (e) the roles of the researcher/participant/audience in generating, analyzing, representing, evaluating, and disseminating the research; (f) approaches to assembling, interpreting, synthesizing, and representing the arts-based content; and (g) methods of dissemination for aesthetic impact and social accessibility. Regardless of the theoretical and methodological approaches to arts-based research, the arts genres (e.g., visual, literary, performative, etc.), and research lenses, all forms of arts in research aim to engage the audience to some degree through the embodied, emotional, and evocative nature of the arts for purposes of providing insight, illumination, and aesthetic resonance (Barone & Eisner, 2012; Cole & Knowles, 2008; Eisner, 2008; Gerber et al., 2020; Gerber & Myers-Coffman, 2018; Kapitan, 2010; Leavy, 2020; McNiff, 2008; Wang et al., 2017).

Overall, these distinctions exist on a continuum relative to the purpose, degree, emphasis, genre, and nature of the inclusiveness of the arts in the research project as well as the role of the researchers/participants/audience in generating, analyzing, evaluating, and disseminating the arts-based data (Archibald & Gerber, 2018; Barone & Eisner, 2012; Cole & Knowles, 2008; Leavy, 2020; McNiff, 2008). Although this continuum presents a range of philosophies, theories, and practices for integrating the arts into research, the importance of the partnership between imaginative mental processes and arts-based practices is the central emphasis and focus for this book.

In addition to the continuum of arts-based research approaches and correlate imaginative mental processes, several researchers have posited the formulation of theoretical concepts and methodological precedents for the integration of imaginative mental processes and arts-based practices into more traditional research approaches and scientific thought including mixed and multi-methods research and hybrid arts/science paradigms (Archibald, 2018; Archibald & Gerber, 2018; Butler-Kisber, 2010; Edwards et al., 2017; Hodgins, 2017). Archibald and Gerber (2018) suggested a gradient continuum describing the arts in the generation, analysis, and integration of data in mixed methods research. They proposed a theoretical model describing how different forms of arts processes and representations enhance and are integrated by varying degrees into singular or multi-phases of the research. Although introduced briefly here, this continuum will be explained in more detail in the chapter devoted to the arts in mixed methods research.

Addressing similar dialectical philosophical constructs and methodological practices, Edwards et al. (2017) theorized the creation of a hybrid of arts and science perspective by "merging artistic and scientific practices in such a way that neither dominates the other [so] . . . artistic and scientific practices can be integrated within a common endeavour, despite the large chasm that is still found between them" (p. 176). Hybrid arts-science approaches call for artist and scientists to disrupt their normal ways of thinking and working. Artists were called upon to systematize their thinking while scientists were asked to dismiss predictive structures or theories in order to discover and construct new knowledge (Edwards et al., 2017). Exemplifying the disruption of usual thinking and implementation of imaginative approaches to research, Edwards et al. (2017) capture the juxta positional arts/science hybrid adventure using the power of imagination and imagery through metaphor: "[w]ith our feet firmly planted in mid-air" (Beckwith & Koukl, 1998, p. 69), and a "willingness to ride multiple, sometimes conflicting waves to find out where they might go" (Caspersen, 2011, p. 94) (p. 182). The use of

Table 1.1 Arts-based research philosophical and methodological continuum

Type	Epistemology	Arts Engagement	Researcher Engagement
Arts-Based Research Practice	Arts-based or aesthetic epistemic	Art as data and investigation Iterative arts processes Singular or multiple arts genres Immersion and reflection Iterative dynamic dialogic analysis Art as result and dissemination Audience engagement and evaluation	Researcher immersion Researcher artistic competence Researcher arts-based responses Participant/researcher Researcher reflection Inclusion of reflection of others Inclusive of evocative imaginal, emotional, sensory, embodied data
Arts-Informed Research	Social constructivist, post-structuralist, post-qualitative, or other qualitative epistemic	Art and qualitative data equally valued Singular or multiple arts genres or exemplars Participant generated arts-based and interview data Exemplifies or amplifies data or results Engagement of audience Qualitatively understood thematically analyzed	Researcher/observer Researcher/participant Researcher collects arts-based data
Arts-Related Research	Social constructivist, pragmatic, or other qualitative epistemic	Art as peripheral data Singular or multiple arts exemplars Participant generated arts-based and interview data Art as illustrative exemplars of qualitative data and/or results	Researcher/observer Researcher collects arts-based data Researcher collects textual data

Source: Reprinted from *Arts-Based Research in the Social and Health Sciences: Pushing for Change With an Interdisciplinary Global Arts-Based Research Initiative* by N. Gerber, E. Biffi, J. Biondo, M. Gemignani, K. Hannes, & R. Siegesmund, 2020, *Forum Qualitative Sozialforschung/Forum: Qualitative Social Research*, 21(2), http://dx.doi.org/10.17169/fqs-21.2.3496. CC BY-4.0

metaphor, the imagery, and the embodied sensations it evokes are illustrative of how the combination of imagination, science, and the arts contribute to the understanding of a holistic human phenomenon and experience. Related to the work of Edwards et al. (2017), Hodgins (2017) studied the integration of the arts and sciences in research and knowledge translation. Acknowledging the usual but productive tensions between scientific accuracy and artistic interpretation, he attempted to illuminate the more subtle "in -between" holistic phenomena of human experience within healthcare. An overarching goal was also to re-visit and review what qualifies as evidence within the arts-based epistemology and the complexity of the creation, translation, and dissemination of new knowledge (p. 226).

In addition to theorizing about the onto-epistemic relationship and tensions between the sciences and the arts, Butler-Kisber and Poldma (2010) have suggested methods for conceptualizing, mapping, and integrating these types of complex and diverse data. They introduced visual inquiry practices in which collage making and concept mapping are a "means for formulating ideas and articulating relationships among these [data] to help understand phenomena in their formative stages" (p. 2). Furthermore, these practices can explore the intricacies of the pre-verbal invisible phenomena concealed in the interstitial spaces "where 'knowledge . . . never arrives . . . it is always on the brink' (Neilsen, 2002, p. 208)" (Butler-Kisber & Poldma, 2010, p. 2).

Along the same lines of using imaginative arts-based inquiry, Gerber and Myers-Coffman (2018) proposed using iterative free association and reverie as a means of accessing pre-verbal intuitive or sense-based embodied forms of knowledge which they identify as an aesthetic epistemology. "wherein previously concealed forms of knowledge emerge, take shape and ultimately facilitate the articulation of our perspectives, the formation of the research question, and decisions about design and methodology" (p. 598).

These perspectives and practices facilitate the incorporation of imagination in research where the convergences and productive collisions of multiple paradigms, methods, and concepts are not only warranted but also encouraged for the investigation and integration of complex data and human phenomena. Summarily, if the arts are to be used as an investigative method of complex human phenomena and for the integration of diverse data sets, then what is meant by the arts and arts-based data, the consideration of the imaginative epistemic, and imaginative arts-based investigative processes, require specific critical exploration and articulation.

References

Abdullah, M. T. (2016). *Metaphorical imagination: Towards a methodology of implicit evidence*. Cambridge Scholars Publishers.

Archibald, M. (2018). Integrating the arts and mixed methods research: A review and a way forward. *International Journal of Multiple Research Approaches*, *10*(1), 342–355. https://doi.org/10.29034/ijmra.v10n1a23

Archibald, M., & Gerber, N. (2018). Arts and mixed methods research: An innovative methodological merger [Special issue]. *American Behavioral Scientist*. Advance online publication. https://doi.org/10.1177/0002764218772672

Barone, T. & Eisner, E. (2012). *Arts based research*. Sage Publications, Inc.

Beckwith, F. and Koukl, G. (1998), *Relativism: Feet Firmly Planted in Mid-Air*, Baker Publishing Group.

Butler-Kisber, L., & Poldma, T. (2010). The poser of visual approaches in qualitative inquiry: The use of collage making and concept mapping in experiential research. *Journal of Research Practice*, *6*(2). Retrieved November 8, 2019 from http://jrp.icaap.org/index.php/jrp/article/view/197/196

Camargo-Borges, C. (2018). Creativity and imagination: Research as worldmaking. In P. Leavy (Ed.), *Handbook of arts-based research* (pp. 88–100). Guilford Press.

Caspersen, D. (2011). 'Decreation: Fragmentation and continuity'. In S. Spier (ed.), William *Forsythe and the Practice of Choreography* (pp. 93–100). Routledge.

Castoriadis, C. (1998). *The imaginary institution of society* (Kathleen Blamey, Trans.). The MIT Press.

Chilton, G., Gerber, N., & Scotti, V. (2015). Towards an aesthetic intersubjective paradigm for arts based research: An art therapy perspective. *UNESCO Observatory Multi-disciplinary Journal in the Arts*, *5*(1), 1–27.

Cole, A.L., & Knowles, J.G. (2008). Arts-informed research. In A.L. Cole and J. G Knowles (Eds.), *Handbook of the arts in qualitative research* (pp. 55–70). Sage Publications, Inc.

Deleuze, G., & Guattari, F. (1987). *A thousand plateaus: Capitalism and schizophrenia*. The University of Minnesota Press.

Edwards, G., Arfaoui, A., McLaren, C., & McKeever, P. (2017). Hybrid health research: Assembling an integrated arts/science methodological framework. *Journal of Applied Arts & Health*, *8*(2). https://doi.org/10.1386/jaah.8.2.175_1

Eisner, E. (2008). Art and knowledge. In J. G. Knowles & A. L. Cole (Eds.), *Handbook of the arts in qualitative research* (pp. 3–12). Sage Publications Inc.

Freud, S. (2017). *Interpretation of Dreams* (A.A. Brill, Trans.). Digireads.com Publishing.(Original work published 1899).

Gemignani, M. (2011). Between researcher and researched: An introduction to countertransference in qualitative inquiry. *Qualitative Inquiry*, *17*(8), 701–708. https://doi.org/10.1177/1077800411415501

Gerber, N. (2020). Saving our soul: Imagination as social activism. In *New directions in theorizing qualitative inquiry*. Myers Education Press.

Gerber, N., Biffi, E., Biondo, J., Gemignani, M., Hannes, K., & Siegesmund, R. (2020). Arts-based research in the social and health sciences: Pushing for change with an interdisciplinary global arts-based research initiative [35 paragraphs]. *Forum Qualitative Sozialforschung/Forum: Qualitative Social Research*, *21*(2). http://doi.org/10.17169/fqs-21.2.3496

Gerber, N., & Myers-Coffman, K. (2018). Translation in arts-based research. In P. Leavy (Ed.), *Handbook of arts-based research* (pp. 587–607). Guilford Press.

Greene, J. C. (2007). *Mixed methods in social inquiry*. Jossey-Bass Press.

Haiven, M., & Khasnabish, A. (2014). *The radical imagination: Social movement research in the age of austerity*. Zed Books Ltd.

Hodgins, M. (2017). An introduction and overview of research knowledge and translation practices in a pan-Canadian arts-based health research study. *Journal of Applied Arts & Health, 8*(2), 225–239. https://doi.org/10.1386/jaah.8.2.225_1

Johnson, R.B. (2015). Dialectical pluralism: A metaparadigm whose time has come. *Journal of Mixed Methods Research, 11*(2), 156–173. doi:10.1177/1558689815607692

Jung, C.G. (1968). *Man and his symbols*. Dell Publishing Company, Inc.

Kapitan, L. (2010). *Introduction to art therapy research*. New York, NY: Routledge.

Klooger, J. (2009). *Castoriadis: Psyche, society, autonomy*. Brill.

Leavy, P. (2020). *Method meets art: Arts-based research practice* (3rd ed.). New York, NY: The Guilford Press.

McNiff, S. (2008). *Art-based research*. In A. Cole & J.G. Knowles (Eds.), Handbook of the arts in qualitative research (pp. 29–40). Sage Publications, Inc.

Montuori, A. (2011). Beyond postnomral times: The future of creativity and the creativity of the future. *Futures, 43*, 221–227.

Neilsen, L. (2002). Learning from the luminal: Fiction as knowledge. *Alberta Journal of Educational Research, 47*, 206–214.

Sardar, Z. (2009). Welcome to postnormal times. *Futures, 42*, 435–444.

Scotti, V., & Gerber, N. (2017). Rendering *beyond words* in transitioning to motherhood through visual and dramatic arts. *Voices: A World Forum for Music Therapy, 17*(3), 1–17. https://doi.org/10.15845/voices.v17i3.924

Springgay, S., Irwin, R. L., Leggo, C., & Gouzouasis, P. (Eds.). (2008). *Being with a/r/tography*. Sense Publications.

St. Pierre, E. (2019). Post-qualitative inquiry in an ontology of immanence. *Qualitative Inquiry, 25*(1), 3–16.4DOI: 10.1177/1077800418772634.

Swan-Foster, N. (2018). *Jungian art therapy: A guide to dreams, images and analytical psychology*. Routledge.

Symington, N. (1996). *The making of a psychotherapist*. International Universities Press Inc.

Urribarri, F. (2002). Castoriadis: The radical imagination and the post-Lacanian unconscious. *Thesis Eleven, 71*, 40–51.

Wang, Q., Coemans, S., Siegesmund, R., & Hannes, K. (2017). Arts-based methods in socially engaged research practice: A classification framework. *Art/Research International: A Transdisciplinary Journal, 2*(2), 5–39.

2 Imagination
Changing worldview and social discourse

In further conducting a critical and articulate exploration of the integration of imaginative mental processes and arts-based practice into research, this chapter focuses on the role of intentional imagination in research at the meta-level contextualized within both dominant research paradigms and the current socio-geo-political landscape. Imagination represents a revolutionary and marginalized paradigm that, in contrast to or concert with more dominant paradigms, can play a transformational role at the meta-level in capturing the nuances and impact of ideological diversity, upheaval, and chaos in these postnormal times (Gerber, 2020; Haiven & Khasnabish, 2014; Klooger, 2009; Montuori, 2011; Sardar, 2009). Klooger (2009) posited that imagination can "conceptualise and elucidate what traditional approaches have distorted and hidden" (p. 4); while Abdullah (2016) invoked metaphorical imagination to illuminate the deeper or invisible connections between the data and the evidence that elude a linear and logical epistemic and correspondent methods.

Social scientists have identified the past several decades as postnormal times (Gerber, 2020; Montuori, 2011; Sardar, 2009). The recent eruption of public outrage has re-exposed the thinly veiled, underlying, and ongoing plague of domination, racism, materialism, and militarism (King as cited in hooks, 1994) in our culture. Therefore, it is a critical time demanding the confrontation of inequitably constructed sociopolitical systems, deconstruction of oppressive racial mythologies and ideologies, reparation of our planet's health, and disassemblage of threats to human health, rights, and regard. These pervasive socio-cultural issues warrant further critical examination, deconstruction, re-construction, and radical change that extend beyond the capacity and limitations of traditional research paradigms (Camargo-Borges, 2018; Haiven & Khasnabish, 2014; Klooger, 2009; Montuori, 2011; Sardar, 2009). The imaginative arts-based onto-epistemic inherently embraces the essential dialectical discourses on the continuum of relevant systemic issues – inclusion, marginalization, domination, oppression, privilege, racism,

DOI: 10.4324/9781003260189-2

sexism, materialism, humanism – creating new insightful perspectives while assigning new values to our culture.

Radical change requires a radical philosophy and strategy. One such strategy is what Castoriadis (1998) called a radical imaginative approach to examining and disrupting the multiple dimensions of previously established but antiquated infrastructures and ideologies (Haiven & Khasnabish, 2014). Haiven and Khasnabish introduced radical imagination as a way of recognizing, reflecting upon, and re-constructing obsolete tacit constructs of our collective cultural unconscious central to how we perceive and participate in our world. According to Castoriadis (as cited in Haiven & Khasnabish, 2014)

> radical imagination is that tectonic, protean substance out of which all social institutions and identities are made, and which, likewise, is constantly in motion under the surface of society, undermining and challenging all that we take to be real, hard, fast, and eternal.
>
> (p. 6)

In this definition, radical imagination is equivalent to the unconscious of society which can be either suppressed or accessed. In this contemporary era, accessing the potential of the unconscious imagination is becoming exceedingly critical to creatively confront what Sardar (2009) calls the "complexity, chaos, and contradictions" of the postnormal (p. 435). According to Montuori (2011), "we are not clear how to think about the future, and how to envision the radical nature of some of the changes that are required" (p. 225). Radical imagination inherently embraces and honors the chaos, uncertainty, and potentiality of the unknown as well as the juxta positioning of difference, tensions, paradox, and upheaval. Therefore, it behooves scholars, scientists, and artists to collaboratively employ imagination and creativity to address these complexities and contradictions, deconstruct the traditional human-made societal constructs and research hegemonies while re-imagining new perspectives, strategies, ideologies, and a global worldview (Camargo-Borges, 2018; Gerber, 2020; Montuori, 2011; Sardar, 2009).

This re-imagining of a global worldview implies that researchers engage in a critical process of evaluating, destabilizing, and recreating tacit assumptions and research paradigms. Harney and Moten (as cited in Klooger, 2009) describe this re-imaging as a convocation or "a process of critical self-reflection, of locating oneself and one's struggles within the multiple intersections of power, and of change and transformation" (p. 17). Camargo-Borges (2018) suggested three critical approaches to deconstructing current assumptions about science and research – the ideological, literary-rhetorical, and the social. The ideological approach posits the assumption that from an objective perspective science investigates singular measurable and generalizable phenomena resulting in the truth. The ideological approach asserts that these assumptions are tainted by underlying systemic biases and stakeholder interests. The second critique is related to the use of language or the limitation of linguistics. Scholars and researchers describe phenomena or theories based upon their own knowledge and worldview, therefore imposing inherent limitations on that knowledge. The final critique refers to the origin of empiricism from a social or cultural context. In other words, the perspectives and methods for identifying what we accept as the truth or factual knowledge are culturally or contextually manufactured and consequently limited (Camargo-Borges, 2018).

Challenging well-established philosophical assumptions also requires courage, vision, and imagination. Haiven and Khasnabish (2014) suggest "to imagine the world, life and social institutions not as they are but as they might otherwise be. It is the courage and the intelligence to recognize that the world can and should be changed" (p. 3). Klooger (2009) concurred suggesting that dominant paradigms have concealed and subjugated worldviews that fundamentalize imagination and its centrality in understanding and sustaining human life. Moten and Harney (as cited in Haiven & Khasnabish, 2014) contend that this subjugation occurs, in part, in the university which is an "artificial and historically particular institution that devalues certain forms of research . . . and exalts others" (p. 12). Responsively, Klooger (2009) proffered that in new paradigms "the imagination/imaginary entails recognising creation as fundamental to the human condition, in both its psychical and social dimensions. That the imaginary, understood as the capacity and activity of positing images/meanings, entails creativity should be obvious" (p. 5).

The acceptance of such assumptions relies upon radical post-modern, post-qualitative, and social constructivist worldviews (Camargo-Borges, 2018; St. Pierre, 2019). Social constructivism is inclusive of imagination and radical imaginative perspectives asserting that truth and reality is an unknown or almost known co-construction emergent within and between people who inhabit the culture and society (Camargo-Borges, 2018; Deleuze & Guattari, 1987; St. Pierre, 2019). "We create, with those around us, multiple, overlapping, contradictory and co-existent imaginary landscapes, horizons of common possibility and shared understanding. These shared landscapes are shaped by and also shape the imaginations and the actions of their participant individuals" (Haiven & Khasnabish, 2014, p. 4).

References

Abdullah, M. T. (2016). *Metaphorical imagination: Towards a methodology of implicit evidence*. Cambridge Scholars Publishers.

Camargo-Borges, C. (2018). Creativity and imagination: Research as worldmaking. In P. Leavy (Ed.), *Handbook of arts-based research* (pp. 88–100). Guilford Press.

Castoriadis, C. (1998). *The imaginary institution of society* (Kathleen Blamey, Trans.). The MIT Press.

Deleuze, G., & Guattari, F. (1987). *A thousand plateaus: Capitalism and schizophrenia.* The University of Minnesota Press.

Gerber, N. (2020). Saving our soul: Imagination as social activism. In *New directions in theorizing qualitative inquiry.* Myers Education Press.

Haiven, M., & Khasnabish, A. (2014). *The radical imagination: Social movement research in the age of austerity.* Zed Books Ltd.

hooks, b. (1994). *Teaching to transgress: Education as the practice of freedom.* Routledge.

Klooger, J. (2009). *Castoriadis: Psyche, society, autonomy.* Brill.

Montuori, A. (2011). Beyond postnomral times: The future of creativity and the creativity of the future. *Futures, 43,* 221–227.

Sardar, Z. (2009). Welcome to postnormal times. *Futures, 42,* 435–444.

St. Pierre, E. (2019). Post-qualitative inquiry in an ontology of immanence. *Qualitative Inquiry, 25*(1), 3–16. https://doi.org/10.1177/1077800418772634

3 Dialectical aesthetic intersubjectivity

A philosophical perspective

In attempts to address the paradigm shift that advocates for the consideration of imaginative onto-epistemologies and arts-based practices in research, a worldview called dialectic aesthetic intersubjectivity is proposed (Archibald & Gerber, 2018; Chilton et al., 2015; Gerber, 2016). The dialectic aesthetic inter-subjective worldview has antecedents in existing paradigms such as social constructivism mentioned in the previous chapter. Additionally, the epistemologies of aesthetics and the ontology of intersubjective pluralism resonate with philosophies of immanence (St. Pierre, 2019), existentialism (Gadamer, 2007; Heidegger, 1976; Levine, 2005), post-structuralism, (Camargo-Borges, 2018; Deleuze & Guattari, 1987), the dialectical stance (Greene, 2007), and dialectical pluralism (Johnson, 2015). In these worldviews, knowledge is a trusted and surprising process that emerges from nothingness and chaos; reflects creativity, multiplicity, and rhizomatic nonlinearity; and is formed and assigned meaning in the dynamic context of pluralistic intersubjectively constructed dialogues (Archibald & Gerber, 2018; Gadamer, 2007; Gerber & Myers-Coffman, 2018; Levine, 2005; St. Pierre, 2019). The dialectic aesthetic intersubjective worldview is also closely aligned with the theoretical derivations of radical imagination that relies upon the creative resources of the unconscious. In the context of radically imaginative psychoanalytic theory, the psyche acts as both drive and representation – energy and meaning (Urribarri, 2002). "Representation is what allows the psyche to imagine: to see something where there is nothing" (Urribarri, 2002, p. 44) and the epistemic of the unknown. The dynamic pluralism of intersubjectivity aligned with a dialectic aesthetic epistemology allows for access, emergence, and insight into the underlying yet invisible precursors of perception and motivators for behavior (Archibald & Gerber, 2018; Chilton et al., 2015; Gerber, 2016; Johnson, 2015). A more in-depth description of the aesthetic epistemology, the pluralistic intersubjective ontology, and the relationship to the integration of imaginative processes and arts-based practices into research is discussed in subsequent sections of this chapter.

DOI: 10.4324/9781003260189-3

The aesthetic epistemology, in this context, is defined using the original Greek meaning – sense-based and perceptual awareness (Cooper, 1997; Gerber, 2020; Harris-Williams, 2010). Sense-based and perceptual awareness reflects the unconscious pre-verbal forms of cognition – sensory, embodied, emotional, and imaginal ways of knowing – which develop and are co-constructed because of dynamic intersubjective communication from infancy and continuing throughout our lifetime (Dissanayake, 2009; Gerber, 2020; Harris-Williams, 2010). In describing the origin of aesthetic intersubjectivity, Hagman (2005) states: "We see its most archaic manifestations in the curve of the mother's shoulder during nursing, her heartbeat and breath, the melody of her voice, the balance of her eyes and smile" (p. 3). Thus, aesthetic intersubjective dialogues develop with our most primal relational communications and fuel our imagination creating the freedom to engage in the playfulness and imaginative narratives ongoing through our lives. Winnicott (as cited in Ogden, 1992) said that these interactions, or aesthetic intersubjective dialogues, that begin in infancy, occur in an imaginal potential space between mother and baby where playfulness becomes the template for creativity and meaningful relationships. Within this dialogic context, the conversations are basically dialectic, allowing for the co-existence and exploration of me and not me, past and present, conscious and unconscious, life and death (Gerber, 2020; Israelstam, 2007; Ogden, 1992). Consequently, aesthetic intersubjective dialogues hold rich histories, artifacts, and memories; and generate personal and collective symbols which are transformed into perpetual and meaningful relational life narratives (Gerber, 2020; Ogden, 1992; Springgay et al., 2008). Engaging imaginatively in research taps into, revives, and reconstructs these aesthetic intersubjective dialogues wherein the concealed artifacts of our life narratives can be retrieved, assembled, and assigned meaning contributing to a more holistic understanding of our personal and collective perceptions and behaviors.

To understand more fully the essential nature of the aesthetic epistemic as we encounter it in research, it may be helpful to explore the historical origins and precedents. Historically, we find precedents and descriptions in Aristotle's (2006) philosophy of aesthetics and Gadamer's (2007) existential adaptation of Aristotle's mechanisms of aesthetics – *poiesis*, *aletheia*, and *energeia* (Archibald & Gerber, 2018; Gadamer, 2007; Levine, 2005). *Poiesis* describes the emergent and existential nature of imagination, creativity, and the arts – "the construction or production of something that did not exist before" (Gadamer, 2007, p. 201). *Poiesis* is the partner in imagination during which the continual dialectical interaction between dynamic forms of aesthetic knowledge at varying levels of consciousness results in the emergence of penetrating insights into the human condition (Gerber & Myers-Coffman, 2018; Levine, 2005, p. 32). As described by Gadamer

(2007), the arts reveal the truth or *aletheia*. "'It comes forth', meaning that the truth 'resides in' the art and becomes 'unconcealed' (Gadamer, 2007)" (Gerber & Myers-Coffman, 2018, p. 593) through the mechanisms of *poiesis* and *energeia*. *Energeia* represents the dynamic psychic and embodied kinetic forces fueling the imaginative creative process propelling the art into existence – driving the *poiesis*. Furthermore, *energeia* "emphasizes the nonlinear, simultaneous, and non-discursive 'motion without path or goal' (Gadamer, 2007, p. 213)" by which *poiesis* and *aletheia* occur (Gerber & Myers-Coffman, 2018, p. 591). *Energeia* also "goes beyond the kinetics of poiesis and the imaginative process, inferring an inherent emotional presence by which 'being aware, seeing or thinking' contributes to the 'unconcealment' of the truth (Gadamer, 1993/2007, p. 213)" (Gerber & Myers-Coffman, 2018, p. 593). These constructs from the philosophy of aesthetics provide insight into the existential nature or emergent process by which truth and knowledge come into being from the chaos of nothingness and through the dynamism of imagination and the arts.

As mentioned previously, aesthetic knowledge is also inherently intersubjective. Its rhizomatic nature (Deleuze & Guattari, 1987) allows the existence in and moving in-between the intersubjective cracks and crevices, the temporal past and present, the relational self and other, and the individual and collective levels of consciousness. The addition of pluralism to aesthetic intersubjectivity refers to the primal and cumulative multiple realities, perspectives, voices, and ambiguities created within human relational phenomena throughout our lifetime (Gerber, 2020). The pluralistic intersubjective ontological aspect of this worldview suggests that since we are born into and live-in constant relationship with other humans, our knowledge is inherently intersubjective. According to Brown (2011), intersubjectivity is a "jointly constructed narrative . . . [that] ascribes meaning to experience for which no language previously existed" (p. 1) and represents a joining on an unconscious preverbal level where "communication and meaning making between two intra psychic worlds . . . results in changes within each member" (p. 109). In other words, when we come together in relationship, we revisit old realities and co-create new ones simultaneously experiencing co-occurring and interactive levels of consciousness and community. Furthermore, the imaginative component of aesthetic intersubjectivity allows us to imagine the other. Psychoanalyst Neville Symington (1996) adds that imagination is the only way we can truly emotionally connect and empathize with another human being. While Haiven and Khasnabish (2014) proffer that it is "intersubjective imagination in which we imagine together, imagine shared stories landscapes and communities collectively" (p. 5). African traditions of aesthetics are inherently intersubjective, spiritual, and communal wherein "the distinction between spectators and participants" is dissolved and the emphasis is on the emergent nature of creativity "from the expressive tradition of the communal canon instead of in response to the reactions of an audience, adoration or wealth" (Welsh-Asante, 1994, p. 3). Therefore, it is posited that through aesthetic pluralistic intersubjective imagination, we can re-interpret the facts of our lives, re-imagine the symbolic constructions, and thus re-write our personal and collective narratives.

As referenced earlier, the potential space is a hypothetical intermediary in-between space wherein dynamic and dialectical interaction between multiple internal psychic and external relational realities occurs. In the theory of potential space, the negotiation between me and not me, subjective and objective, naturally occurs through a dynamic dialectical process of joining, play, and creativity resulting in the formation of metaphor, symbolization, and personal narrative (Ogden, 1992, p. 205). Furthermore, the potential space provides a theoretical concept by which the symbol and the symbolized are created resulting in the capacity for the individual to "view his [*sic*] thoughts, feelings, perceptions, and behavior as constructions, as opposed to impersonal registrations of fact" (Ogden, 1992, p. 117).

The concept of potential space, referencing the intimate pre-verbal dialogues between humans, can be applied to research by attuning to the aesthetic knowledge expressed within the intersubjective contexts of researcher/participant or what Gemignani (2011) calls between the researcher and the researched. It is postulated that by attending to these aesthetic intersubjective communications in the liminal spaces within multiple relational research contexts, diverse and tacit forms of data are revealed contributing to enhanced insight into the phenomena being investigated.

One example of the use of aesthetic data generated in the liminal or intersubjective space in research was described by Gemignani (2011). He addressed the potential space between researcher and researched as a source of rich sensory and emotional data in qualitative interviews that became essential to understanding the phenomenon under investigation. In other words, the countertransference or the "emotional field" which is co-created between the researcher and the participant becomes a rich data source that re-creates and induces in the researcher the authentic intersubjective experience of the participant. "I realized that the participants' narrations would have lost meaning and interpretability without the emotional reactions they generated in the teller as well as in me, the listener" (Gemignani, 2011, p. 701). The honoring of the potential space and the valuing of the co-constructed aesthetic narratives that emerge in the joining of realities and emotional communication between researcher and participant has implications not only for enhancing the understanding of the phenomenon, but also for redefining the nature of the relationships and power dynamics in both art and research. The reconsideration of these relationships embraces the difference, values paradox and questions, honors the other, and allows for the researcher, participant, artist, and audience to engage with equal voices. As exemplified in traditions such as African aesthetics, the investigation becomes more dialogic and communal eliminating researcher and researched or artist and audience disparities (Welsh-Asante, 1994).

The assumptions in this worldview posit that the human condition and human motivation can be understood more holistically through including the study of dialectical aesthetic forms of knowledge residing in and emerging from our pluralistic intersubjective realities informed by and co-existent with our histories and levels of consciousness. Furthermore, this worldview includes and values the induced aesthetic relational experience of the researcher and participant(s) in the creative potential space as data essential to comprehensively understanding the phenomena under investigation while redefining relationship and equal voice in the research process. These ways of knowing and being would otherwise be inaccessible using more typical or logical forms of inquiry but become accessible through engaging imaginative mental processes and arts-based practices as forms of conceptualization and investigation (Gerber, 2020).

A critical discussion of these onto-epistemological perspectives is precursory and essential to shifting from the typical ways of thinking about research to those that involve imagination and inclusiveness by integrating diverse ways of knowing with pluralistic realities and methodologies. As asserted by hooks (1994), we must confront the "politics of domination" in the academy where "unnecessary and competing hierarchies of thought" are established to create restrictive standards of excellence, acceptability, or inferiority of scholarly works (p. 64). The dialectic aesthetic intersubjective worldview joins others which have attempted to challenge the hegemony of dominant research paradigms. Perspectives such as radical imagination (Haiven & Khasnabish, 2014), the dialectical stance (Greene, 2007), and dialectical pluralism (Johnson, 2015) emphasize the tensions of difference as essential knowledge sources creating space for the revelation of paradoxical modes of unconscious, imaginative, and aesthetic ways of knowing within pluralistic co-constructed intersubjective realities. Within these perspectives' dynamic psychic knowledge, diverse social realities and multiple voices can co-exist and co-create with imaginative inclusivity. "Indeed, as Justin Paulson (2010) notes, on a phenomenological level the imagination is the product of difference: it is sparked and grows when we encounter the unexpected, the foreign, the new" (Haiven & Khasnabish, 2014, p. 7).

Summarily, the concepts of poiesis, dynamism, symbolism, and inter- and intrapsychic constructivist dialogues at various levels of consciousness contribute to the dialectical aesthetic epistemic and pluralistic intersubjective ontology in a worldview of imagination. This onto-epistemological perspective facilitates a critically reflective rupture of typical binaries and embedded modes of thinking by introducing imaginative ways of conceptualizing and understanding the human experience; and by proposing creative radical methodologies that accurately capture and represent the complexity of the human condition (Edwards et al., 2017; Eisner, 2008; Gerber, 2020; Haiven & Khasnabish, 2014; Kapitan, 2010). Such extreme disruptions of accepted wisdom and the introduction of new, sometimes uncomfortable ways of thinking require us to engage in conscious collective reflection and imagine beyond what we think we know. As explained by Sardar (2009):

> Given that our imagination is embedded and limited to our own culture, we will have to unleash a broad spectrum of imaginations from the rich diversity of human cultures and multiple ways of imagining alternatives to conventional, orthodox ways of being and doing.
>
> (p. 443)

References

Archibald, M., & Gerber, N. (2018). Arts and mixed methods research: An innovative methodological merger [Special issue]. *American Behavioral Scientist*. Advance online publication. https://doi.org/10.1177/0002764218772672

Aristotle. (2006). Poetics (M. E. Hubbard, Trans.). In D. Cooper (Ed.), *Aesthetics: The classic readings* (pp. 29–44). Blackwell Publishers Ltd.

Brown, L. J. (2011). *Intersubjective processes and the unconscious: An integration of Freudian, Kleinian, and Bionian perspectives*. Routledge.

Camargo-Borges, C. (2018). Creativity and imagination: Research as worldmaking. In P. Leavy (Ed.), *Handbook of arts-based research* (pp. 88–100). Guilford Press.

Chilton, G., Gerber, N., & Scotti, V. (2015). Towards an aesthetic intersubjective paradigm for arts based research: An art therapy perspective. *UNESCO Observatory Multi-disciplinary Journal in the Arts*, *5*(1), 1–27.

Cooper, D. E. (Ed.). (1997). *Aesthetics: The classic readings*. Blackwell Publishing.

Deleuze, G., & Guattari, F. (1987). *A thousand plateaus: Capitalism and schizophrenia*. The University of Minnesota Press.

Dissanayake, E. (2009). The artification hypothesis and its relevance to cognitive science, evolutionary aesthetics and neuroaesthetics. *Cognitive Semiotics*, *5*, 148–173. www.ellendissanayake.com/publications/

Edwards, G., Arfaoui, A., McLaren, C., & McKeever, P. (2017). Hybrid health research: Assembling an integrated arts/science methodological framework. *Journal of Applied Arts & Health*, *8*(2). https://doi.org/10.1386/jaah.8.2.175_1

Eisner, E. (2008). Art and knowledge. In J. G. Knowles & A. L. Cole (Eds.), *Handbook of the arts in qualitative research* (pp. 3–12). Sage Publications Inc.

Gadamer, H. G. (2007). The artwork in word and image: "So true, so full of being". In R. E. Palmer (Ed.), *The Gadamer reader: A bouquet of later writings* (pp. 192–224). Northwestern University.

Gemignani, M. (2011). Between researcher and researched: An introduction to countertransference in qualitative inquiry. *Qualitative Inquiry, 17*(8), 701–708. https://doi.org/10.1177/1077800411415501

Gerber, N. (2016). Mixed methods research and art therapy. In D. Gussak & M. Rosal (Eds.), *The Wiley-Blackwell handbook of art therapy* (pp. 654–662). Wiley-Blackwell.

Gerber, N. (2020). Saving our soul: Imagination as social activism. In *New directions in theorizing qualitative inquiry*. Myers Education Press.

Gerber, N., & Myers-Coffman, K. (2018). Translation in arts-based research. In P. Leavy (Ed.), *Handbook of arts-based research* (pp. 587–607). Guilford Press.

Greene, J. C. (2007). *Mixed methods in social inquiry*. Jossey-Bass Press.

Hagman, G. (2005). *Aesthetic experience: Beauty, creativity and the search for the ideal*. Rodopi B.V.

Haiven, M., & Khasnabish, A. (2014). *The Radical Imagination: Social Movement Research in the Age of Austerity*, London, UK: Zed Books, Ltd.

Harris-Williams, M. (2010). *The aesthetic development: The poetic spirit of psychoanalysis*. Karnac Books.

Heidegger, M. (1976). The origin of the work of art. In A. Hofstadter & R. Kuhns (Eds.), *Philosophies of art & beauty: Selected readings in aesthetics from Plato to Heidegger* (pp. 3–67). The University of Chicago Press.

Hooks, B. (1994). *Teaching to transgress: Education as the practice of freedom*. Routledge.

Israelstam, K. (2007). Creativity and dialectical phenomena: From dialectical edge to dialectical space. *International Journal of Psychoanalysis, 88*, 591–607.

Johnson, R. B. (2015). Dialectical pluralism: A metaparadigm whose time has come. *Journal of Mixed Methods Research, 11*(2), 156–173. https://doi.org/10.1177/1558689815607692

Kapitan, L. (2010). *Introduction to art therapy research*. Routledge.

Levine, S. K. (2005). The philosophy of expressive arts therapy: *Poeisis* as a response to the world. In P. J. Knill, E. G. Levine, & S. K. Levine (Eds.), *Principles and practice of expressive arts therapy: Towards a therapeutic aesthetics* (pp. 15–74). Jessica Kingsley Publishers.

Ogden, T. (1992). *The matrix of the mind: Object relations and the psychoanalytic dialogue*. Karnac Books.

Paulson, Justin. 2010. 'The Uneven Development of Radical Imagination'. *Affinities: A Journal of Radical Theory, Culture, and Action, 4*(2): 33–38.

Sardar, Z. (2009). Welcome to postnormal times. *Futures, 42*, 435–444.

Springgay, S., Irwin, R. L., Leggo, C., & Gouzouasis, P. (Eds.). (2008). *Being with a/r/tography*. Sense Publications.

St. Pierre, E. (2019). Post-qualitative inquiry in an ontology of immanence. *Qualitative Inquiry, 25*(1), 3–16. https://doi.org/10.1177/1077800418772634

Symington, N. (1996). *The making of a psychotherapist*. International Universities Press Inc.

Urribarri, F. (2002). Castoriadis: The radical imagination and the post-Lacanian unconscious. *Thesis Eleven, 71*, 40–51.

Welsh-Asante, K. (Ed.). (1994). *The Africa aesthetic: Keeper of the traditions*. Praeger.

4 Imagination in research

Reconceptualizing method, data, and evidence

In the dialogue between thoughts and writing I am constantly bombarded by images, emotions, and sensations related to what I am attempting to express. I wish there was a way to record these images in my mind -- formative and intuitive precursors to the language and their correlate ideas which I struggle to articulate. They are the manifestation of the dynamism of free association, visualization, and improvisation forming pulsating interactive colors and threads of a tapestry weaving a not quite visible story; or they are the flashing images of a light through a film strip forming a Morse code of patterns. These pulsations and patterns transform from sensations or pre-image to pictures almost like the lens of a camera coming into focus. I can feel them and see them and almost touch them they are just out of reach --the preverbal, embryonic, aesthetic forms of cognition. I see the gaps in the knowledge as empty spaces where images might fill in and weave together the diverse shapes and colors, numbers, and words, creating a new story. But I enjoy and engage with the moment trusting that these sensations will be born and grow into metaphors and symbols, words, and phrases, leading me to where I want to go or to where I never expected or intended to go. Nonetheless they are responsive to and dialogic with the central concepts I am attempting to study, construct, and convey. Many of us may have these experiences but perhaps they remain out of our consciousness, so we do not attend to or develop them. Or perhaps we even dismiss them as a distracting nuisance or noise. I am proposing that these are essential forms of data which need more intentional attention and cultivation in order to enhance the texture, depth and insight of research. So here is where the ideas of metaphor and symbol enter research as the bridges between internal imaginational sensory, embodied, and preverbal nascent ideas and the construction of the imaginal and correlational language.

DOI: 10.4324/9781003260189-4

Throughout this book, the onto-epistemic of imagination and the practices of arts-based research have been introduced as a challenge to the basic assumptions of scientific traditions in the spirit of shifting paradigms, expanding thought, and considering diverse practices. Intersubjective ontologies, aesthetic eclecticism, dialecticism, and methodological pluralism guide our thinking beyond the limitations of scientific empiricism and into the realm of imagination (Archibald, 2018; Chilton et al., 2015; Gerber & Myers-Coffman, 2018; Greene, 2007; Johnson, 2015). The use of imagination and the arts can address the complexities of human phenomena filling the spaces left within and between more traditional forms of data and results while stretching the disseminative reach and impact. But the integration of imaginative processes and arts-based methods challenges us to think beyond existing paradigms and critically examine the underlying research constructs of typologies, practices, and terminology. Challenging, re-envisioning, and re-creating such embedded constructs is in itself an imaginative process which will be discussed in this chapter.

Edwards et al. (2017) suggested that as artistic inquiry enters the dialogue with traditional scientific research perspectives and practices, we begin to acknowledge that "novelty is created through deterritorializations and rhizomatic processes, through recognition and acknowledgement of the Other, and recognition and acknowledgement of limitations. This process of shifting the ground is why the process involved is sometimes called anti-method" (p. 182). Implicit in this discussion of shifting paradigms and anti-methods is the critical consideration of how or if the basic research concepts and terminology such as method, data, and evidence need to be redefined and linguistically reconstructed. Such considerations also require a thorough assessment of the implications from dramatic re-imaginings and re-constructions of such embedded dominant structures. There is some current interest in and radical movement toward challenging the overall relevance of the constructs, such as method, data, and evidence, to innovative and imaginative research approaches. Abdullah (2016) speaks to "the never letting go of the challenges of social research practice, alongside a growing need for parallel sensemaking options to review complexity and deception in contemporary evidence – the story of our times" (p. 12). Similarly, Hodgins (2017) acknowledges that the "growing use of art-based knowledge creation and translation strategies is driving an important shift in the understanding of what counts as evidence, and appreciation for the complexity and multidimensionality involved in creating new knowledge" (p. 226). Perhaps in response to these challenges, St. Pierre (2019) proposed "an ontology of immanence from poststructuralism as well as transcendental empiricism [which] . . . is methodology-free" (p. 3). Transcendental empiricism, according to Deleuze (1994), is based in aesthetics when we "apprehend directly in the sensible that which can only be sensed, the very being *of* the sensible: difference, potential difference and difference in intensity as the reason behind qualitative diversity" (pp. 56–57). Vagle and Hofsess (2016) spotlight post-intentional phenomenology in which they infuse Deleuze and Guattari's (1980/1987) "notion of lines of flight and situate it in connection with other of their important notions such as *assemblage, multiplicities, and rhizome*" (Vagle & Hofsess, 2016, p. 334). Post-intentionality here captures the dynamic, pluralistic, and rhizomatic nature of human connectedness and meaning making and perhaps aspires to transcendental empiricism. These innovative perspectives engage us in peeling away embedded tacit structures that have dominated research thought and practice revealing what might have been oppressed and concealed while illuminating new perspectives, marginalized diverse voices and knowledge types, and the inclusiveness of difference and creativity.

Seemingly new and innovative, these ideas are not without historical precedents that have implored the re-evaluation and deterritorialization of staid research traditions in favor of imaginative paradigms and innovative research structures. For instance, Gadamer (2003) proffered that the human sciences were existential and phenomenological by nature, thus acknowledging the limits of applying principles of scientific empiricism. Gadamer advocated for the equal consideration of the "emotive, imaginative reflections and intuitive" (as cited in Abdullah, 2016, p. 4) that could only be studied inductively to "arrive at their conclusions through an unconscious process" (Gadamer, 2003, p. 5). In 1931, Edmund Husserl (as cited in Moustakas, 1994), the phenomenological philosopher, invoked the use of the intuitive and the imaginative in research.

> [T]he pure essence, can be exemplified intuitively in the data of experience, data of perception, memory, and so forth, but just as readily in the play of fancy we bring spatial shapes of one sort or another to birth, melodies social happenings and so forth, or live through fictitious acts of everyday life.
>
> (Moustakas, 1994, p. 98)

Based upon Husserl's principles, Moustakas (1994) proffered the use of what he called "imaginative variation" as a phenomenological research method in which "there is a free play of fancy; any perspective is a possibility and is permitted to enter into consciousness" (p. 98).

Embracing these historical precedents and imaginative perspectives necessitates the critical re-consideration of traditional research constructs. Such a critical reflexive process requires the courage to engage in uncomfortable and disconcerting confrontations with basic familiar assumptions and safe structures, upon which we have heretofore relied, to tell us not just what we know or what we think we know, but more importantly what we do not know. Imagining beyond what we know, how we know, or how or who we are exposes and uproots many of our entrenched belief systems at the essential core of our being catapulting us into the boundless space of the unknown. The unknown is fraught with the dizzying anxiety of uncertainty, fears of emptiness, disorientation, and existential premonitions of death while simultaneously filled with new possibility, spirituality, soulfulness, creativity, knowledge, and life (Abdullah, 2016; VanDusen, 1999; Welsh-Asante, 1994). In Eastern philosophy, the concept of the unknown, often representing the life–death dialectic, has been referred to as the no-mind, the fertile void, or the creative center (Israelstam, 2007; VanDusen, 1999). Although considered a precipice of opportunity in Eastern philosophy, Western thought and research hegemonies can compel us to want to hastily fill the void to mitigate the anxiety of the unknown with what we already know; but the rush to fill the void may circumvent opportunities and obfuscate the truth. By sitting with the emptiness, meditating on it, and engaging with its disparities, confusions, and paradoxes, new insights can be created (Van Dusen, 1999). The unknown is part of the imaginative epistemic. Imaginative thinking and related arts-based processes can accommodate, tolerate, and embrace the tensions of the unknown while maximizing the creative potential of the fertile void. Trusting in and valuing imaginative and arts-based processes such as *poiesis, energeia, and aletheia* can increase our patience and practices, inform our understanding of multiple forms of data, look beyond the obvious and convenient, value emergence over prediction, engage in the dialectics of difference, and allow for the emergence, contemplation on, and interpretation of multiple types of knowledge in research.

Living with uncertainty, the unknown and yet-to-be revealed situating us on the creative "dialectical edge" (Israelstam, 2007, p. 594) has been the world and role of artists for centuries. Perched on that dialectical edge, artists have been the original researchers or explorers of the-not- yet-known (St. Pierre, 2019) confronting, blank pages, empty canvases, vacant stages, and silent melodies – imagining what could be, engaging in creative dialogues, plumbing the depths of the soul, and giving birth to new ideas. St. Pierre (2019) cites Lyotard's (1983/1988) concept of the *differend* which is the "unstable state and instant of language wherein some Thing which must be able to be put into phrases cannot yet be (p. 13)" (p. 3). William James referred to similar ideas in different language acknowledging the importance of "states of insight into depths of truth unplumbed by the discursive intellect. They are illuminations, revelations, full of significance and importance, all inarticulate though they remain; and as a rule, they carry with them a curious sense of authority" (as cited by the Institute of Noetic Sciences, 2018).

Setting the stage with these current trends, historical precedents, and onto-epistemic fundamentals related to the infusion of imaginative perspectives into research allows us to return to considering how method, evidence, and data are redefined, generated, and evaluated within an imaginative onto-epistemic and arts-based research practice context. Based upon the previous discussion, we can begin to see that in imaginative processes and arts-based research practices, we are interested in mindfully engaging with the chaos and nothingness of the unknown, the not-yet-known (St. Pierre, 2019) simultaneously acknowledging and maximizing the *dialectic, aesthetics, intersubjectivity, rhizomes, and multiplicitous* forms of knowledge that might previously have been labeled "noise" in traditional research paradigms and likely dismissed. With these perspectives in mind, we can begin re-examining the central concepts and terms in research to determine if re-conceptualizing and re-naming is warranted. We begin with the term and concept of data. The traditional definition of data references visible, tangible, and measurable facts. The consistent premises in the definition of data are the reference to factual knowledge and typically numerical knowledge upon which certain assumptions and calculations are based. Based upon these defining characteristics, it seems that this term is restricted to specific types of knowledge within the physical and statistical realm while excluding other forms of knowledge within the imaginative realm. Abdullah (2016) notes and questions this disconnect during her own research:

I could not endorse the emergence of my insights, and equally was unable to let the data speak through the norms of data citation, because a fluidity in such emergent insights could hardly be held together and reported as valid evidence in the data.

(p. 3)

In facing this dilemma about applying the concept of physical data to more elusive and invisible ways of knowing, Abdullah (2016) discovered that when challenged with "making sense of data complexity, metaphor proved robust and offered coherence" (p. 6). Abdullah (2016) addresses and breaks out how the complexity and convergence of social-linguistic, ideational-ideological, historical, cultural, and institutional contexts (p. 5) impose multiple and interdependent meanings on descriptive phrases that cannot be wholly or authentically captured, interpreted, or portrayed by singular data-driven evidence-based constructs. Thus, the multi-dimensional spatio-temporal qualities of metaphor and symbolism become relevant forms that can capture, make visible, and in some ways physicalize these more elusive forms of data or knowledge, in textual, visual, embodied, or other aesthetic genres of knowledge. Rumbold (2014) concurs when differentiating the types of knowledge generated by the arts from more traditional generalizable scientific evidence. The "objective evidence" from the sciences, although presumed to represent the most efficacious in healthcare, is actually not always equated with desirable of therapeutic outcomes (Rumbold, 2014). The arts, which are socially constructed, contribute the nuanced and empathic human context, amplifying our insights and understanding of the human condition necessary for health and healing. Furthermore, the arts "provide a fresh perspective that curbs our tendency to stereotype and encourages imaginative responses. Such engagement also nurtures our capacity for affective responses to life and enables us to discover our interior landscape (Eisner, 2008, pp. 10, 11)" (Rumbold, 2014, p. 265).

Perhaps in taking this discussion further, we might entertain Spinoza's (as cited in Hallett, 2013) contestation of the assumptive absolutism of physical or factual data. Spinoza posited that the concepts of ideas and *ideata* hold the truth which is in the mental action or within the inherent nature of ideas, both terminally and attributably (p. 59).

> We have seen that an idea is not true by reason of its congruence with "fact": . . . . The certification of truth must lie within the nature of ideas, "facts" being established by the truth of ideas, and not the truth of ideas by appeal to "facts".
>
> (Hallett, 2013, p. 60)

Thus, the term data typically refers to enumeration and facts, while *ideata* infers more internal and imaginative mental processes; perhaps we can shift our terminology to be inclusive of both *data* and/or *ideata* to more precisely identify and differentiate the forms of knowledge we use and seek.

Continuing this exploration of tacit research terms and structures, Abdullah (2016) examined the complexities of data and their relationship to evidence. She argues that it is the researcher's job to "find evidence in data and not data in evidence and be able to discover any [critical] underlying relationships between the data and evidence" (p. 4). But these assertions and relationships are dependent upon how we define, regard, and understand data and evidence. Abdullah (2016) suggests that the term evidence, as the root word tells us, refers to that which is seen thus excluding that which is unseen.

> Evidence has a weight;
> Evidence has a body, or perfect body;
> Evidence is hard or soft; weak or strong;
> Evidence is prima facie and corpus delicti.
>
> (p. 6)

Conversely, that which is unseen, covered, invisible, or unclear when discovered, uncovered, and revealed is typically not considered evidence because of the basic intangible properties (Abdullah, 2016, p. 7). The deconstruction of these constructs is critically relevant to developing a case for defining and valuing the imaginative onto-epistemic in research particularly since these forms of knowledge such as physical, measurable, or visible data and evidence have been assigned superior value and a privileged truth. Contrarily, unseen ideas, perceptions, sensations, feelings, or visualizations, the aesthetic knowledge of imagination, and the essential complex human experience are often assigned minimal or no value in research. If we consider that this assignation of value is based on different knowledge characteristics rather than a hierarchical determination of veracity, we can conclude that imaginative and ideational knowledge is no less significant or important but rather different in their essential nature from physical, objective, or seen evidence (Rumbold, 2014).

Thus, in re-considering concepts of evidence and data, metaphor and symbol serve as a legitimate substitute compatible with the complexities and nature of the ideational, invisible, unknown imaginative onto-epistemic (Abdullah, 2016; Gerber & Myers-Coffman, 2018). Metaphor and symbolism are viable representatives and conduits of complex ideas existing beyond the physical, linear, and measurable. Metaphors, linguistic equivalents of symbolism, are capable of capturing essential multi-dimensional and paradoxical ideas and phenomena in a condensed form. The nature of metaphor "lends itself to the mining of the imagination, unearthing and depicting archaic sensory and embodied artifacts, assembling and constructing intricate stories – stories that hold and represent rich and multiple meanings which are otherwise inaccessible" (Gerber & Myers-Coffman, 2018, p. 596). Based upon this reasoning, Abdullah (2016) introduced "metaphor as a schema that allows researchers to reinterpret evidential complexities around them . . . for the utilisation of metaphor as a cognitive methodology" (p. 13). Abdullah's (2016) conceptual and methodological innovation, called metaphorical imagination (MI), suggests a reconfigured and revalued concept of implicit, ideational, reflective data as equally credible contributors to knowledge. "MI allows embodied cognition of empiricism and intuitivism – the body and soul of evidence" (p. 13). Abdullah (2016) argues that the soul, as revealed through metaphor, provides insight into multiple dimensions of the individual, cultural, and systemic phenomena otherwise inaccessible. She asks why the metaphor

> could not be taken into account by the empiricist norms and protocols and serve as a credible source of evidence. Hence, it became clear, that, only because the soul was not physical and visible, the exclusively positivist norms would disregard its potential utility.
>
> (p. 8)

Suggesting a new linguistic affiliated with invisible and soulful data, Abdullah (2016) further contends that "if evidence is cognitively conditioned to have a physical body, could we not correspondingly uncondition or recondition evidence in an implicit soul?" (p. 8). Addressing these epistemic differences as part of her metaphorical imaginational paradigm, Abdullah (2016) identifies several new dimensions of and parameters for unseen evidence:

- Where and when the evidential settings are likely to be complex, uncertain, and deceptive;
- Where and when the evidential settings are figurative and likely to be insufficient to rationalise in an empirical and literal sense;
- Where and when evidential settings are likely to reveal hidden meanings across experiential-intersubjective and interpretative-intertextual analyses; and
- Where and when, in terms of serendipitous, heuristic, and reflexive sensemaking of implicit contexts, the tacit influence is likely to become cognitively viable.

(p. 15)

These perspectives on ideata, metaphor, and symbol as concepts and related terminology that more accurately capture the complex nature of beingness and knowledge residing in the imaginative onto-epistemic allow us to adopt an approach to non-evidence, anti-method, and metaphorical imagination as innovative practices and knowledge translators (Abdullah, 2016).

Further adding to the authenticity and credibility of these ways of knowing, theorizing, and categorizing is the study of symbolism representing the individual/collective mind and the cultural consciousness. The domains of philosophy, psychoanalysis, sociology, and anthropology have inherently valued signs, visualizations, metaphors, and symbols which are regarded and posited to be the visible manifestations of the invisible imagination and the unconscious (Innis, 1985; Jung, 1968; Swan-Foster, 2018). Certainly, anthropologists have been studying the biological, cultural, and linguistic history of humans through signification in semiotics – signs in language, thought, and symbols – over the past 150 years and beyond. "Human civilization is dependent upon signs and systems of signs, and the human mind is inseparable from the functioning of signs – if indeed mentality is not to be identified with such functioning" (Morris as cited in Innis, 1985). More recently, symbolic interactionism, which emphasizes creativity, "accentuates how individuals create and recreate their social worlds through the use and manipulation of symbols in a joint interaction with co-social actors in a dynamic and infinite fashion" (Quist-Adade, 2019). Furthermore, anthropological and psychoanalytic perspectives consider cultural and individual systems of signification, symbolic thought, and preverbal communication, or what we are calling an aesthetic epistemic, as a biological and cultural intersubjective imperative

> wherein aesthetics is considered a relational way of knowing, beginning in early mother-child pre-verbal communications and contributing

to the development of our lifelong experience of human relationality, beauty, and empathy (Chilton et al., 2015; Dissanayake, 2009; Gerber et al., 2012; Hagman, 2011; Harris-Williams, 2010; Kapitan, 2010; Springgay et al., 2008).

(Gerber & Myers-Coffman, 2018, p. 593)

From these perspectives, we know that the intangibility of thought, its relationship to the perception of human mind, and its manifestations in language, speech, image, symbol formation, and intersubjective meaning assignation have long intrigued scholars and been the object of study (Hallett, 2013; Innis, 1985; Vygotsky, 2012). In particular, symbols have been considered the multi-dimensional carriers of personal and collective histories, the bridge between the unconscious and the conscious, a condensation of co-existent past and present, the holders and purveyors of the secrets of our personal, intersubjective, and cultural narratives (Jung, 1969; Swan-Foster, 2018). Symbols are dynamically co-created and re-created in a dialectical space in between people, levels of consciousness, time and space generating meaning for us personally and collectively. The symbol "allows for the signification and representation of ambiguous, illusive, invisible, partially or not fully known phenomena that are inexpressible in words (Hinz, 2009; Lusebrink, 1990)" (Gerber & Myers-Coffman, 2018, p. 596). Constructed from multiple sensory, embodied, emotional, imaginal pre-verbal content, the symbol provides access to rich memories and artifacts within a compact space representing simultaneity, multiplicity, and transcending spatio-temporality. Consequently, symbols and their cousin metaphors have the capacity to capture and represent the *complexity, emergent dynamism, paradoxical dialectics, intersubjectivity, rhizomes, and multiplicity* central to defining the onto-epistemic of imagination, the practice of arts in research, and ultimately, revealing the nuances of the human condition.

Finally, symbolism and related aesthetics also carry an implicit axiological component in the imaginative onto-epistemic, the socially accessible impact of arts-based research, and socially responsible philosophy of radical imagination. Within these contexts and research approaches, a brief mention of the ethical issues associated with the elicitation of imaginative and symbolic thoughts as ideata/data is warranted. Symbols are often the product of history, experience, and perception, the total meaning of which is not readily apparent. Stored in the unconscious with the meaning partially concealed, symbolism has the power to insidiously manipulate and dictate personal and cultural attitudes and traditions that form, permeate, and influence our perceptions and behaviors often outside of our awareness. A cultural example of this phenomenon is offered by Welsh-Asante (1994), who describes the impact of Eurocentric aesthetics in which "light and dark as good and evil, which established the dichotomy of essential characteristics of white and black aesthetic and the concept of superior versus inferior beauty" (p. 8). These values which have existed unquestioned for centuries have implicitly defined how we perceive and treat one another based upon color distinctions. Symbolic thought and its manifestation in the arts thus carry ideata that shape our culture and ultimately inform our personal and collective beliefs and behaviors. Symbols are a rich source of ideata/data emanating from our individual and collective imagination which impact our embedded belief systems. When symbols are carefully investigated, respecting the power of their partially unknown and concealed nature, they can reveal insights contributing to a more holistic understanding of our history, culture, morality, and behavior.

Symbol and metaphor are the harbingers and representations of the elusive soulful or ideational data living within the imaginative onto-epistemic awaiting revelation. Within this imaginative onto-epistemology, symbol and metaphor epitomize and capture the qualities of *emergent dynamism, paradoxical dialectics, intersubjectivity, rhizomes, simultaneity, and multiplicity* essential for unpacking insight and making meaning. With meaning emerging through and between internal reflection and external intersubjective dialogues, symbolic and metaphorical constructs begin to form and assemble from fragmentary sensory, embodied, and emotional or aesthetic ideata, reveal, and illuminate the invisible yet essential aspects of the human experience (Abdullah, 2016; Deleuze & Guattari, 1980/1987; Gerber & Myers-Coffman, 2018; Hodgins, 2017; Kapitan, 2010). Making these invisible forms of implicit data visible (Mersch, 2015; Swan-Foster, 2018) is the challenge facing contemporary imaginative and arts-based researchers wherein the traditional representations of physical evidence alone are insufficient to represent the holistic human experience of the mind and soul.

Accessing the ideata/data, and ultimately evidentiary, counterparts of symbols and metaphors essential for the construction of new knowledge and insights is the work of the imaginative arts-based researcher and perhaps that of the mixed methods researcher adopting imaginative and arts-based approaches. The investigative practices include circuitous emergent free associations, reflections, improvisation, mental and actual image making revealing the formative sensory, embodied, and emotional precursors and artifacts that may be considered the equivalent of data. Additional practices might include circumambulation and active imagination, which in Jungian psychoanalysis refers to the "devotional practices" circling and awakening images illuminating the truth or our individual and collective unconscious (Swan-Foster, 2018, p. 28). These emergent images "pique our curiosity and invite us to decipher" (Swan-Foster, 2018, p. 28).

When these aesthetic artifactual data equivalents or ideata are assembled in metaphoric and symbolic representations, they reveal previously concealed aspects of our individual and collective unconscious lives. Through such approaches, the artifacts emerge from the unconscious, symbols and metaphors form, meanings are assigned, and, our now conscious narratives are re-constructed resulting in insight into and understanding of the human phenomena under investigation.

As referenced previously, Haiven and Khasnabish (2014) view imagination, or "the realm of 'the imaginary' (l'imaginaire) where ideas, meanings, associations, fixations, drives and affects circulate beneath the threshold of conscious thought (see Urribarri, 2002)" (p. 5). Existing on individual, and intersubjective unconscious levels, imagination initiates curiosity and the use of productive tensions when encountering surprises, the unusual, or difference (Camargo-Borges, 2018; Haiven & Khasnabish, 2014). The use of collective and individual imaginative thinking allows access to and understanding of complex paradoxical human phenomena, diverse forms of data and ideata, and behavior inaccessible and unexplainable through empirical science. However, the concepts and constructs of dominant research paradigms require re-evaluation for their applicability, translation to, and maximization of the imaginative processes and arts-based practices in research. Camargo-Borges (2018) suggested that imagination in research allows for the formation of new images, new vision, new scenarios emergent from notions and developing into fully formed ideas leading to impactful change (p. 93). Therefore, by employing intentional imaginative processes, we can re-conceptualize the usual research linguistics and typologies of method, data, and evidence to be more compatible with the proposed imaginative onto-epistemology. Sensory, embodied, emotional, and imaginal knowledge is the language of the collective unconscious and potential correlates of data. The intentional imaginative and systematic retrieval, assemblage, iterative deconstruction and re-construction into linguistic and arts-based forms such as metaphors and symbols, evidentiary equivalents, provide new and much needed practices, meaning, and syntheses for exploring and explaining the elusive workings of the human individual and collective psyche.

References

Abdullah, M. T. (2016). *Metaphorical imagination: Towards a methodology of implicit evidence.* Cambridge Scholars Publishers.

Archibald, M. (2018). Integrating the arts and mixed methods research: A review and a way forward. *International Journal of Multiple Research Approaches, 10*(1), 342–355. https://doi.org/10.29034/ijmra.v10n1a23

Archibald, M., & Gerber, N. (2018). Arts and mixed methods research: An innovative methodological merger [Special issue]. *American Behavioral Scientist.* Advance online publication. https://doi.org/10.1177/0002764218772672

Camargo-Borges, C. (2018). Creativity and imagination: Research as worldmaking. In P. Leavy (Ed.), *Handbook of arts-based research* (pp. 88–100). Guilford Press.

Chilton, G., Gerber, N., & Scotti, V. (2015). Towards an aesthetic intersubjective paradigm for arts based research: An art therapy perspective. *UNESCO Observatory Multi- disciplinary Journal in the Arts*, *5*(1), 1–27.

Deleuze, G. (1994). *Difference and repetition* (P. Patton, Trans.). Columbia University Press.

Deleuze, G., & Guattari, F. (1987). *A thousand plateaus: Capitalism and schizophrenia*. The University of Minnesota Press.

Dissanayake, E. (2009). The artification hypothesis and its relevance to cognitive science, evolutionary aesthetics and neuroaesthetics. *Cognitive Semiotics* (5), 148–173. Retrieved from http://www.ellendissanayake.com/publications/

Edwards, G., Arfaoui, A., McLaren, C., & McKeever, P. (2017) Hybrid health research: Assembling an integrated arts/science methodological framework. *Journal of Applied Arts & Health*, *8*(2). https://doi.org/10.1386/jaah.8.2.175_1

Eisner, E. (2008). Art and knowledge. In J. G. Knowles & A. L. Cole (Eds.), *Handbook of the arts in qualitative research* (pp. 3–12). Sage Publications, Inc.

Gadamer, H. G. (2003). *Truth and method* (2nd ed., J. Weinsheimer & D. G. Marshall, Trans.). The Continuum International Publishing Group Inc.

Gerber, N., & Myers-Coffman, K. (2018). Translation in arts-based research. In P. Leavy (Ed.), *Handbook of arts-based research* (pp. 587–607). Guilford Press.

Gerber, N., Templeton, E., Chilton, G., Cohen-Liebman, M.S., Manders, E., Shim, M. (2012). Art based research as a pedagogical approach to studying intersubjectivity in the creative arts therapies. *Journal of Applied Arts & Health, 3*(1), 39–48.

Greene, J. C. (2007). *Mixed methods in social inquiry*. Jossey-Bass Press.

Hagman, G. (2005). *Aesthetic experience: Beauty, creativity, and the search for the ideal*. Amsterdam, Netherlands: Rodopi. B.V.

Haiven, M., & Khasnabish, A. (2014). *The radical imagination: Social movement research in the age of austerity*. Zed Books Ltd.

Hallett, H. F. (2013). *Benedict De Spinoza: The elements of his philosophy*. Bloomsbury Academic.

Harris-Williams, M. (2010). *The aesthetic development: The poetic spirit of psychoanalysis*. London: Karnac Books.

Hinz, L. D. (2020). *Expressive therapies continuum: A framework for using art in therapy* (2nd ed.). Routledge.

Hodgins, M. (2017). An introduction and overview of research knowledge and translation practices in a pan-Canadian arts-based health research study. *Journal of Applied Arts & Health*, *8*(2), 225–239. https://doi.org/10.1386/jaah.8.2.225_1

Innis, R. E. (1985). *Semiotics: An Introductory Anthology*. Indiana University Press.

Israelstam, K. (2007). Creativity and dialectical phenomena: From dialectical edge to dialectical space. *International Journal of Psychoanalysis*, *88*, 591–607.

James, W. (2018, August 8). *The Institute of Noetic Science*. https://noetic.org/about/noetic-sciences/

Jung, C.G. (1968). *Man and his symbols*. Dell Publishing Company, Inc.

Jung, C. G. (1969). *Man and his symbols*. Doubleday.

Kapitan, L. (2010). *Introduction to art therapy research*. Routledge.

Lusebrink, V. B. (1990). *Imagery and visual expression in therapy*. Plenum Press.

Lyotard, J.-F. (1988). *The differend: Phrases in dispute* (G. Van Den Abbeele, Trans.). Minneapolis: University of Minnesota Press. (Original work published 1983).

Mersch, S. (2015). *Epistemologies of aesthetics*. Diaphanes.

Moustakas, C. (1994). *Phenomenological research methods*. Sage Publications Inc.

Quist-Adade, C. (2019). *Symbolic interactionism: The basics*. EBSCO Publishing ebook collection.

Rumbold, B. (2014). Evidence in practice: Nurturing aesthetic reflexivity. *Journal of Arts and Health*, *5*(1), 263–271.

Springgay, S., Irwin, R. L., Leggo, C. & Gouzouasis, P. (Eds.). (2008). *Being with a/r/tography*. Sense Publications.

St. Pierre, E. (2019). Post-qualitative inquiry in an ontology of immanence. *Qualitative Inquiry*, *25*(1), 3–16. https://doi.org/10.1177/1077800418772634

Swan-Foster, N. (2018). *Jungian art therapy: A guide to dreams, images and analytical psychology*. Routledge.

Urribarri, F. (2002). Castoriadis: The radical imagination and the post-Lacanian unconscious. *Thesis Eleven*, *71*, 40–51.

Vagle, M. D., & Hofsess, B. A. (2016). Entangling a post-reflexivity through post-intentional phenomenology. *Qualitative Inquiry*, *22*(5), 334–344. https://doi.org/10.1177/1077800415615617

Van Dusen, W. (1958/1999). Wu-Wei No-Mind, and the fertile void in psychotherapy. In A. Molino (Ed.) *The couch and the tree: Dialogues in psychoanalysis and Buddhism* (pp. 52–57). North Point Press.

Vygotsky, L. (1934/2012). *Thought and Language* (revised edition). MIT Press.

Welsh-Asante, K. (Ed.). (1994). *The Africa aesthetic: Keeper of the traditions*. Praeger.

5 Imaginative processes and arts-based practices in research

Overview of imaginative processes and arts-based practices in research

Throughout the book, the dialectical aesthetic intersubjective worldview has been posited as a way of being, knowing, and thinking about imagination and its tangible representative in the arts. This worldview holds multiple dimensions and types of aesthetic – sensory-embodied, ambiguous, symbolic, and dynamic – knowledge reflective of the collective intersubjective human experience normally residing outside of the limits of traditional modes of thought and investigation. These onto-epistemics make imaginative arts-based forms of inquiry applicable to the investigation and integration of multiple forms of diverse phenomena and ideata/data. Essential and optimal to including the arts in research, particularly in the integration and synthesis of diverse data, is defining and practicing them as an imaginatively driven process. Therefore, from this perspective, imaginative processes and correlate arts-based practices are centralized as the primary approaches to investigation. Imaginatively driven arts-based inquiry may include intentional, spontaneous, and strategic iterative in-depth practices such as free association, improvisation, reflection, deconstruction, and assemblage, and symbolic synthesis within a dynamic intersubjective dialogic context. In this section, we will explore imaginative-driven arts-based research practices along with the roles of participants and roles/competencies of the researcher.

Imaginatively driven processes and arts-based investigational practices depend upon the dynamic interaction and iterations between intention and improvisation, immersion and reflection, formation and assemblage, deconstruction, and integration relative to particular questions and phenomena. These imaginative processes and arts-based practices result in the generation of new ideata/data as well as for the transformational integration of these ideata/data resulting in a meaningful final synthesis. Imaginative

DOI: 10.4324/9781003260189-5

arts-based practices may involve: (a) eliciting formative sensory-embodied impressions and images by engaging in evocative free associative and mindful reveries; (b) improvisational use of single or multiple arts-based genres to develop ideas; (c) intentional and strategic use of artistic media/ genres to enhance, intensify, clarify, or synthesize phases of conceptualization, ideata/data generation, in-depth investigation, analysis, and synthesis; (d) juxta positioning, assembling, and capitalizing on the dialectical tensions of difference between pre-logical sensation, visualization, and imagery with logical language and measure; and (e) varying degrees of researcher/ participant/audience involvement in artistic ideata/data generation, dialogue, investigation, analysis, synthesis, evaluation, and representation. More specific examples of these iterative, reflective, and investigative imaginatively driven arts-based practices include free association and reverie; spontaneous arts-based responses; intersubjective improvisations, dialogues and formations; arts-based assemblages, narrations, and concept mapping; intersubjective arts-based dialogic deconstructions and re-assemblages; formation of symbols and metaphors; and interpretation, synthesis, representation, and dissemination (Butler-Kisber & Poldma, 2010; Chilton & Scotti, 2014; Gerber & Myers-Coffman, 2018; Leavy, 2015; Manders & Chilton, 2013; Sajnani, 2013). Artistic genres and mediums used in these processes may include one or more of the following: visual arts, (e.g., collage, painting, drawing, sculpture), fiction prose and poetry, drama, dance, music, multimedia, and other art forms. The implementation of imaginative processes, arts-based procedures, and the intentional selection of arts-based genres may depend upon the nature of the topic under investigation; the phase of the research; the strategies for further in-depth investigation or amplification; the need for symbolization, clarification, and integration of ideata/data under analysis; and the artistic competency of the investigator(s).

The artistic mind: artistic competencies of the researcher

The artistic competency of the investigator is critical for the engagement with imaginative and arts-based research requiring further discussion. Due to the uniqueness, unfamiliarity, and in some ways awkwardness of approaching research within the imaginative and arts-based onto-epistemic, exploration of the aptitudes or competencies of the researcher is warranted. In addition to more traditional research skill, in imaginative arts-based research approaches, the researcher may need aptitudinal competence including new ways of attending, attuning, thinking, and knowing. In other words, the multi-determined, rhizomatic, and intersubjective nature of imaginative investigations requires an artistic mind and worldview. The artistic mind refers to the capacity for: attunement, engagement, and reflection within and between the imaginative arts process and the participant; attentiveness to free associative wanderings; tolerance and receptivity to the unknown, ambiguity, and the dialectical dialogue; and the paradigmatic shift of the multiple roles of the researcher as participant, artist, and investigator. The researcher in these instances needs to be attuned to the unconscious, pre-linguistic, pre-logical, or aesthetic forms of knowledge that emerge and meander around and through the in-between intra- and intersubjective spaces. The attunement and sensitivity to these invisible, intersubjective, ambiguous aesthetic, or sensory-embodied forms of knowledge initially drive the intuitive iterative and dialogic arts-based investigation. This investigation leads to the formation, assemblage, and transformation of emergent aesthetic artifacts into symbols, metaphors, and meaning (Archibald & Gerber, 2018; Deleuze & Guattari, 1987; Gadamer, 2007; Gerber & Myers-Coffman, 2018; Greene, 2007; Johnson, 2015; Springgay et al., 2008, p. 86; Van Dusen, 1999).

Implicit in the descriptions of the researcher artistic mind and mentality in imaginative process, arts-based research practice is the centrality of intersubjectivity. This perspective encompasses the concept that knowledge is co-created within the undeniable interdependent and relational context from which new perspectives and narratives emerge. As Gemignani (2011) observes:

> The co-creation of knowledge is especially salient in emotionally intense inquiries that engage the researcher at an intimate and subjective level and that doom any attempt to maintain an attitude of detached scientism. Such a personal involvement enriches the rapport with participants and contributes to data constructions and interpretations.
>
> (p. 702)

Through this lens, the researcher may need to reflect upon and/or adjust their perception of the relationship between the researcher and the phenomenon, researcher and the participant, the researcher and the art, and the researcher and the audience. These adjustments are to assess implicit oppressive or power dynamic relational attitudes, tacit dominant research perspectives or biases, unconscious content, the aesthetic power of the art, and practices that may impede or obscure the emergence of the authentic co-construction of knowledge about the research phenomena. During these reflections, which can be reveries, arts-based and/or dialogic, the researcher can attune, attend to, and explore the artifactual ideata/data hidden in the intersubjective crevices that emerge dialogically "in-between" the researcher, co-researchers, and participants, the researcher/artist and the researched/art, the art and the ideata/data, and the community and the audience.

Concomitant to these reflections and attitudinal adjustments, as per Gemignani's (2011) observations, is the researcher's capacity to remain present and receptive to the emerging emotional, sensory-embodied, paradoxical, and symbolic phenomena generated in the potential spaces throughout encounters with participants, the artistic inquiry, the audience, and oneself. Intentionally, and perhaps temporarily, setting aside the familiar positioning of the logical objective scientific mind, the artistic mind openly immerses itself to capturing emergent, unfiltered, pre-verbal phenomena and reflections through imaginative processes and arts-based practices central to understanding, constructing, and collectively assigning meaning to the arts-based ideata/data and symbolic synthesis within the lived inter- and intrasubjective context. Most importantly, the researcher needs to develop a respectful awareness of the power of the arts as a form of revelatory investigation in that it unearths surprising phenomena from the individual and collective unconscious which can be both exciting and disconcerting for the researcher, participants, and audience.

Because of the unconscious nature, multi-dimensionality, and aesthetic power of imaginative processes and arts-based practices, it may be useful to recruit a research team including co-researchers who possess the aptitudes and skills necessary to engage competently in the various generative, reflective, and synthetic phases of the research. Within these researcher roles, a team can provide diverse imaginative perspectives and experiences, arts-based competencies, intersubjective reflections, and interpretative co-processing of the ideata/data. The collaborative team dialogues and arts-based exchanges are critical to the identification of the unconscious artifacts, aesthetic and emotional resonance; essential meaning assignation; relevance and verisimilitude; and evocative power of the arts-based results that extend beyond one individual. In this way, the arts-based research team can also consider not only the authenticity of the result but also the ethical implications of the work with regard to its ultimate impact on researchers, participants, and the audience.

Imaginative processes and arts-based practices at different phases of research

The integration of imaginative processes and arts-based practices can occur at multiple phases, at critical junctures, and in various ways during the conduct of the research. The researcher and/or research team can consult to make critical decisions about at which phase or phases the integration of imaginative mental processes and arts-based practices might occur during the research. The specific imaginative processes and arts-based practices used may depend upon the phase of the research, the intention of process, and the arts-based proclivities of the researcher or research team. For instance, in the formative conceptual stages of the research, imaginative and arts-based processes may be used to mine unknown or emergent ideas, elicit the not-quite-formed, use random shape, color, sound, or movement to create a reflective dialogue, and coax the nascent notions into being. Processes such as free association, doodling, random color, shape and movement creations, poetic, dance, music, or dramatic intersubjective improvisations begin the conversation with the unconscious and the unknown or not-yet-known and soon-to-be-born (Dixon, 2013; Gerber & Myers-Coffman, 2018; Learmonth & Huckvale, 2013; Sajnani, 2013; St. Pierre, 2019). These processes engage in ways of knowing that promote "opening to uncertainty and embracing instability" (Sajnani, 2013, p. 81) allowing for the "simultaneity and fluidity of knowledge that co-exists between people and within the researcher . . . immersion in and thinking about" (Learmonth & Huckvale, 2013, p. 98). The arts processes represent a complex ecosystem in which "embodied levels of art-making" and "imagined sensations" contribute to the imagination and the emergence of the idea (Learmonth & Huckvale, 2013, p. 106).

Imagination and arts-based practice can also be used in the ideata/data generation phases either as researcher responses to the data being generated or as a method to enhance the in-depth meaning of the ideata/data provided by participants. Arts-based responsive mark/movement/sound-making, memoing, assembling and re-assembling ideata/data (Gerber & Myers-Coffman, 2018; Learmonth & Huckvale, 2013), storying textual or statistical data, textual description and recontextualizing imaginative variation (Moustakas, 1994), intersubjective data-driven dialogues or performances (Sajnani, 2013) are all practices that can enhance understanding of the ideata/data being generated determining emergent directions for the research. Furthermore, Kapitan (2010) suggests varying iterations of seeing through constructs, reflections on strategies, creative dialogues, and questions and contexts (p. 172) as approaches to data generation using arts-based practices. Writing a play to help re-conceptualize the basic constructs emerging in the data; creating poetic or dramatic dialogues between the research question, phenomena, and emergent data; keeping visual, poetic, or musical reflections on the data; and using visual, literary, and other art forms inherently stimulate active engagement with and re-imagining of the emerging data. Used throughout all phases of the research, these imaginative and arts-based explorations can sustain the degree of emotional attunement and presence of the researcher(s) while exploring and integrating the invisible yet influential, thus essential, aesthetic intersubjective communications between researchers, researcher and participant, researcher and audience.

Similarly, in analysis and integration phases, imagination and arts-based practices are useful when one needs to understand the relationships between multiple diverse and intersectional forms of convergent and divergent knowledge. When addressing phases of data analysis or, as in arts-based language, phases of translation (Gerber & Myers-Coffman, 2018; Manders & Chilton, 2013) imaginative arts-based processes can be used to engage in deductive and inductive thinking (Learmonth & Huckvale, 2013) braided metaphoric processes (Sullivan, 2010, p. 113) and/or collaging and concept/pictorial mapping (Butler-Kisber & Poldma, 2010). These imaginative processes and arts-based practices allow for the dynamic interaction between arts-based and other research traditions such as critical, empirical, and interpretivist approaches transcending paradigmatic boundaries (Sullivan, 2010, p. 100). For instance, through imaginative processes, the researcher can shift lenses and use arts-based practices to explore differences/tensions between pre-existing data-driven empiricist and problem identification perspectives; the interpretivist view of finding and making meaning through creation and co-construction; and/or the critical theory perspective using "dialectical and deconstructive methods" giving voice to marginalized peoples through "cyclical creating and critiquing" (Sullivan, 2010, p. 106). Using imaginative and arts-based approaches such as collage and concept or pictorial mapping, tearing apart and re-constructing, moving around and filling spaces, movement and dramatic enactments, pictorial, poetic, or musical storying can provide new analytic and integrative perspectives through re-aligning, juxtaposing, re-visualizing, and re-configuring paradigmatic and ideata/data relationships (Butler-Kisber & Poldma, 2010; Manders & Chilton, 2013).

Imaginative processes arts-based practices such as this value and include aesthetic or preverbal sensory-embodied emotional and imaginal knowledge that disrupt usual thinking, shape new emergent ideas, embrace ambiguity, deconstruct, assemble, and transform ideata/data resulting in syntheses in metaphors and symbols. The resulting symbols and metaphors provide a vehicle for condensing, assembling, merging, and connecting diverse and ambiguous forms of ideata/data transcending the restrictions of time, space, and usual logic allowing for the emergence of new perspectives and meaning. Selecting and using these approaches as intentional and strategic aspects of the research design and procedures pose intriguing possibilities and potential creative outcomes.

References

Archibald, M., & Gerber, N. (2018). Arts and mixed methods research: An innovative methodological merger [Special issue]. *American Behavioral Scientist.* Advance online publication. https://doi.org/10.1177/0002764218772672
Butler-Kisber, L., & Poldma, T. (2010). The poser of visual approaches in qualitative inquiry: The use of collage making and concept mapping in experiential research.

Journal of Research Practice, *6*(2). Retrieved November 8, 2019 from http://jrp. icaap.org/index.php/jrp/article/view/197/196

Chilton, G., & Scotti, V. (2014). Snipping, gluing and writing: The properties of collage as an arts-based research practice in art therapy. *Art Therapy: Journal of the American Art Therapy Association*, *31*(4), 163–171.

Deleuze, G., & Guattari, F. (1987). *A thousand plateaus: Capitalism and schizophrenia*. The University of Minnesota Press.

Dixon, J., Fenner, P., & Rumbold, P. (2013). The risks of representation: Dilemmas and opportunities in art-based research. In S. McNiff (Ed.), *Art as research: Opportunities and challenge* (pp. 67–78). Intellect Ltd.

Gadamer, H. G. (2007). The artwork in word and image: "So true, so full of being". In R. E. Palmer (Ed.), *The Gadamer reader: A bouquet of later writings* (pp. 192–224). Northwestern University.

Gemignani, M. (2011). Between Researcher and Researched: An Introduction to Countertransference in Qualitative Inquiry. *Qualitative Inquiry*, *17*(8), 701–708. DOI: 10.1177/1077800411415501.

Gerber, N., & Myers-Coffman, K. (2018). Translation in arts-based research. In P. Leavy (Ed.), *Handbook of arts-based research* (pp. 587–607). Guilford Press.

Kapitan, L. (2010). *Introduction to art therapy research*. Routledge.

Learmonth, M., & Huckvale, K. (2013). The feeling of what happens: A reciprocal investigation of inductive and deductive processes in an art experiment. In S. McNiff (Ed.), *Art as research: Opportunities and challenge* (pp. 97–108). Intellect Ltd.

Leavy, P. (2015). *Method meets art: Arts-based research practice*. The Guilford Press.

Manders, E., & Chilton, G. (2013). Translating the essence of dance: Rendering meaning in artistic inquiry of the creative arts therapies. *International Journal of Education & the Arts*, *14*(16), 1–17.

Moustakas, C. (1994). *Phenomenological research methods*. Sage Publications, Inc.

Sajnani, N. (2013). Improvisation and art-based research. In S. McNiff (Ed.), *Art as research: Opportunities and challenges* (pp. 79–85). Intellect Ltd.

Springgay, S., Irwin, R. L., Leggo, C., & Gouzouasis, P. (Eds.). (2008). *Being with a/r/tography*. Sense Publications.

Sullivan, G. (2010). *Art practice as research: Inquiry in visual arts* (2nd ed.). Sage Publications Inc.

Van Dusen, W. (1958/1999). Wu-Wei No-Mind, and the fertile void in psychotherapy. In A. Molino (Ed.), *The couch and the tree: Dialogues in psychoanalysis and Buddhism* (pp. 52–57). North Point Press.

6 Imagination and integration in mixed and multi-method research

The principles and practices reiterated throughout this book will now be discussed specifically in the context of integration in mixed and multi-methods research. The philosophical assumptions, imaginative processes, and arts-based practices have been described previously, so in this chapter the focus is, first, to briefly review philosophical contexts and apply them to the overall concept of integration in mixed and multi-methods research; and, second, to demonstrate the comparison and alignment of specific integrative approaches with imaginative and arts-based practices. It is posited that the addition of onto-epistemologically relevant imaginative processes and correlate arts-based practices provide the requisite mindset and mechanisms for conceptualizing, revealing, and integrating paradigmatic and data diversity. It is worth noting that although the concept of integration in research has typically been associated with mixed and multi-method research, imaginative processes and arts-based practices could conceivably be integrated into other research traditions.

The integration of qualitative and quantitative data in mixed methods research is central to its aspirational mission to increase the diversity, depth, authenticity, robustness, and holism in the investigation of particular phenomena (Bazeley, 2016; Creswell & Plano Clark, 2011; Fielding, 2012; Greene, 2007; Guetterman & Fetters, 2018). Despite dominant binary either–or research thinking, which inherently resists integrating statistics with text or measure with meaning, Bazeley (2016), citing Gorard, reminds us that any "phenomenon, whether physical, emotional, or cognitive, intrinsically has both qualities and quantity" (p. 190). Implicit in this reminder is the necessity of a paradigm shift committed to comprehensively re-examining and studying the complex and multiple dimensions of diverse forms of qualitative and quantitative knowledge disruptive of the binary. As referenced previously, in attempts to accommodate and initiate this paradigm shift, mixed methods and arts-based researchers have constructed several creative and innovative worldviews including the dialectical stance (Greene,

DOI: 10.4324/9781003260189-6

2007), dialectical pluralism (Johnson, 2015), and dialectical aesthetic inter-subjectivity (Chilton et al., 2015). Furthermore, theories of post-intentional phenomenological lines of flight (Vagle & Hofsess, 2016), post-qualitative inquiry's immanent ontology and anti-method (St. Pierre, 2019), radical imagination's social unconscious (Haiven & Khasnabish, 2014), and rhizomatic post-structuralist thinking (Deleuze & Guattari, 1987) lead us in ways of thinking far beyond the binary opening to possibility in the imaginative realm. In these worldviews, the philosophical assumptions, re-envision radical and imaginative ways of engaging with multi-dimensional knowledge, pluralistic realities, and multi-data/ideata research assigning primacy to transformative and integrative investigative and analytic practices.

These established worldviews embrace innovative perspectives and research approaches by inviting the addition of imaginative processes and arts-based practices to existing integrative methods. Within these contexts, Greene (2007) encourages "a spirit of adventure" (p. 144) in research, requiring a prying loose from singular myths of predictability and generalizability and moving into the realm of unknown possibility. Re-thinking such embedded research myths and methods, to make room for imaginative processes and arts-based approaches in research, requires an intentional, mindful, and reflective practice to deconstruct and reconceptualize the usual premises for research. Re-imagining those principles and tenets that we have tacitly taken to be true includes the reconsideration and valuation of underlying unconscious liminal ideata/data that contribute to the construction, understanding, and illumination of multiple meanings from diverse perspectives (Haiven & Khasnabish, 2014; Klooger, 2009; Montuori, 2011; Sardar, 2009; Urribarri, 2002). As asserted by Fielding (2012):

> Its search for the single valid "finding" acts against the truly radical potential that mixed methods research has to build prismatic understandings of social phenomena and to promote the analytic density from which iterative social knowledge can be built.
>
> (p. 125)

Furthermore, in the intentional and reflective countering, the "single valid finding" while introducing the multi-dimensional pluralistic nature of imaginative arts-based approaches to integration in research, we may need to consciously re-imagine the tacit underlying premises or structures that might be misaligned with and obstructive to more creative explorations. For instance, in a previous chapter, the intentional reconsideration and renaming of constructs, such as data, evidence, and method was proposed to radically transform embedded structures using (Abdullah, 2016; Archibald & Gerber, 2018; Fielding, 2012) a conscious "creative innovation and a conceptualizing rather than pragmatic approach" (Fielding, 2012, p. 126). Such transformative considerations initiate the imaginative process opening to new possibilities, meanings, and insights through the revelation and integration of previously concealed or marginalized knowledge.

With the intentional and reflective re-defining of implicit research structures, imaginative and arts-based practices focus on conceptualization, visualization, imagination, and illumination beyond the usual, tangible, and obvious. These imaginative mental processes accompanied by arts-based practice resemble and rely upon a previously referenced concept of *poiesis*. *Poiesis* refers to the existential emergence, contemplation, and formation of previously unknown notions born from the unconscious or not-quite-known resulting in the creation of something new. These not-quite-known notions are often hidden in the intersubjective crevices and the liminal spaces of diverse and divergent ideata/data. In imaginative processes and arts-based practices, these forms of ideata/data are prioritized through valuing reflection and contemplation; facilitating dialectic dialogues; revealing and juxta positioning illusive ideata/data; actively exploring and elaborating on the tensions of difference; re-formulating and re-imagining ideata/data relationships; forming metaphors and symbols; assembling, integrating, and synthesizing; and illuminating meaning and insight (Archibald & Gerber, 2018; Bazeley, 2016; Gadamer, 2007; Greene, 2007; Johnson, 2015).

Translating these ideas into mixed and multi-method research, Bazeley (2016) emphasizes the often-ignored presence of tacit qualitative meaning in statistical and numerical data which can contribute to further illumination of *almost known* aspects of the phenomenon. Greene (2007) further posits that imaginative and creative processes are necessary alternatives to uncon-cealing these concealed and reluctant aspects of data and the truth. Greene reiterates the relevance and power of metaphor as a translational creative process in dynamic analyses to reveal invisible ideata, integrate a diverse data, and illuminate holistic insights. She proffers that these processes and meanings "are not so much readily apparent in analytic results as they are inferred and interpreted by the inquirer as he or she engages in the work of data analysis" (p. 142). Imagination and arts-based approaches are suited for the exploration and exposure of tacit knowledge or invisible or concealed data existing in the liminal spaces between qualitative and quantitative, researcher and researched, symbol and symbolized.

Traditional approaches to integration mixed methods research are categorized in several ways. Creswell and Plano Clark (2011) identify and define integration in the three processes of *merging, connecting, and building* depending upon the mixed methods research design. Merging is typically used in convergent designs when the data are placed side-by-side using joint visual displays or other forms of comparison. Connecting refers primarily to explanatory sequential designs wherein the statistical results are converted into categories or themes that inform the sampling and exploratory parameters for the qualitative phase. Building refers to the construction of quantitative variables and instruments based upon qualitative thematic results in an exploratory sequential design (Creswell & Plano Clark, 2011; Guetterman & Fetters, 2018). Other authors have introduced additional albeit similar concepts with regard to the integrative process in mixed methods research. Pluye et al. (2018) studied multiple authors' strategies for integration and categorized them as *connection, comparison,* and *assimilation.* In their model, *connection* relates to "*sequential development* (Bazeley, 2009), *correlation and comparison* (Greene, 2007), or *sequential mixed analysis* (Teddlie & Tashakkori, 2009)" (p. 44). *Comparison* speaks to the processes of "*triangulation and expansion* (Bazeley, 2009), *joint inferential analysis* (Greene, 2007), or *parallel analysis* (Teddlie & Tashakkori, 2009)" (p. 44). Finally, *assimilation* refers to "*transformation* (Bazeley, 2009), *transformation and consolidation* (Greene, 2007), and *mixed analysis conversion* (Teddlie & Tashakkori, 2009)" (p. 44). Greene (2007) and Teddlie and Tashakkori (2003, 2009, 2010) further identify three overarching principles inherent in these integrative processes which are "complementarity, dialectical tension, and unification" (Pluye et al., 2018, p. 44). These principles are both present across integrative categories and essential to obtaining the most robust results.

Within the context of these traditional integrative approaches, precursors to the use of more intentional imaginative mental processes and related arts-based practices have been used in forms of visualization and graphic representations. Some of these practices originated in the traditions in the social sciences. Particularly, ethnographic and case study research has included implicit mixing of methods and merging of qualitative and quantitative data through the use of repertory grid analysis, social network analysis, and its offspring in visual graphing, and Q methodology (Bazeley, 2016). Furthermore, the emergence of geo-referencing software and principles, visual streaming, and joint displays offer additional innovative visual methods of integrating diverse forms of data particularly in mixed methods research (Fielding, 2012; Guetterman & Fetters, 2018). Touching on more imaginative integrative processes Greene (2007) describes the procedures of data cleaning, reduction, transformation, and correlation. In Greene's description, the most imaginative thinking seems to occur in the phase of transformation where methods of narration, symbolization, visual displays are used to reveal and amplify the qualitative and quantitative aspects of their counterparts.

Speaking more specifically to arts-based practices aligned with explorative and integrative phases in mixed methods research, Archibald and Gerber (2018) suggested that the arts might contribute a new dimension and aspirational insight when used in mixed methods research as either an additional or integrative strand. They conceptualized the arts in research as existing on a continuum depending upon the type and phase of research, the type of arts genre, the source of the arts-based data, the role of the researcher, the degree to which the art is an integral aspect of generation and analysis of the data, and the positioning of the arts within the research. The authors proposed four categories of arts integration into mixed methods research:

> (a) communicative integration (e.g., using the arts to communicate about mixed methods findings through dissemination), (b) data source integration (e.g., using the arts to gather data for use in a mixed methods study, often by way of visual elicitation), (c) analytical integration (e.g., using the arts in analysis, or as a complementary reflexivity strategy), and (d) conceptual integration (e.g., using arts at the level of ABR, where ABR and MMR are positioned as mutually informative, interwoven components of the overall design).
>
> (p. 2)

The previous examples use various degrees of imaginative arts-based practices in conceptualization, visualization, data generation and analysis, and integration for different purposes and at various phases of the research. However, not all of these examples feature or emphasize the imaginative mental processes combined with arts-based practices that act not only to represent but also to investigate, reveal, transform, and integrate the ideata/ data. Imaginative processes and arts-based practices specifically for integration in mixed methods research will be elaborated in the next chapter.

References

Abdullah, M. T. (2016). *Metaphorical imagination: Towards a methodology of implicit evidence*. Cambridge Scholars Publishers.

Archibald, M., & Gerber, N. (2018). Arts and mixed methods research: An innovative methodological merger [Special issue]. *American Behavioral Scientist*. Advance online publication. https://doi.org/10.1177/0002764218772672

Bazeley, P. (2009). Analysing mixed methods data. In S. Andrew & E. J. Halcomb (Eds.), *Mixed methods research for nursing and the health sciences* (pp. 84–118). Chichester, England: Wiley.

Bazeley, P. (2016). Mixed or merged? Integration as the real challenge for mixed methods. *Qualitative Research in Organizations and Management: An International Journal, 11*(3), 189–194. https://doi.org/10.1108/QROM-04-2016-137

Chilton, G., Gerber, N., & Scotti, V. (2015). Towards an aesthetic intersubjective paradigm for arts based research: An art therapy perspective. *UNESCO Observatory Multi- disciplinary Journal in the Arts, 5*(1), 1–27.

52   *Imagination and integration*

Creswell, J. W., & Plano Clark, V. L. (2011). *Designing and conducting mixed methods research* (2nd ed.). Sage Publications Inc.

Deleuze, G., & Guattari, F. (1987). *A thousand plateaus: Capitalism and schizophrenia*. The University of Minnesota Press.

Fielding, N. G. (2012). Triangulation and mixed methods designs: Data integration with new research technologies. *Journal of Mixed Methods Research, 6*(2), 124–136. https://doi.org/10.1177/1558689812437101

Gadamer, H. G. (2007). The artwork in word and image: "So true, so full of being". In R. E. Palmer (Ed.), *The Gadamer reader: A bouquet of later writings* (pp. 192–224). Northwestern University.

Greene, J. C. (2007). *Mixed methods in social inquiry*. Jossey-Bass Press.

Guetterman, T., & Fetters, M. (2018). Two methodological approaches to the integration of mixed methods and case study design: A systematic review. *American Behavioral Scientist, 62*(7), 900–918.

Haiven, M., & Khasnabish, A. (2014). *The radical imagination: Social movement research in the age of austerity*. Zed Books Ltd.

Johnson, R. B. (2015). Dialectical pluralism: A metaparadigm whose time has come. *Journal of Mixed Methods Research, 11*(2), 156–173. https://doi.org/10.1177/1558689815607692

Klooger, J. (2009). *Castoriadis: Psyche, society, autonomy*. Brill.

Montuori, A. (2011). Beyond postnomral times: The future of creativity and the creativity of the future. *Futures, 43*, 221–227.

Pluye, P., Bengoechea, E. G., Granikov, V., Kaur, N., & Tang, D. L. (2018). A world of possibilities in mixed methods: Review of the combinations of strategies used to integrate qualitative and quantitative phases, results and data. *International Journal of Multiple Research Approaches, 10*(1), 41–56.

Sardar, Z. (2009). Welcome to postnormal times. *Futures, 42*, 435–444.

St. Pierre, E. (2019). Post-qualitative inquiry in an ontology of immanence. *Qualitative Inquiry, 25*(1), 3–16. https://doi.org/10.1177/1077800418772634

Tashakkori, A., & Teddlie, C. (2010). *Handbook of mixed methods in social and behavioral research* (2nd ed.). Thousand Oaks, CA: Sage.

Teddlie, C., & Tashakkori, A. (2003). Major issues and controversies in the use of mixed methods in the social and behavioural sciences. In A. Tashakkori & C. Teddlie (Eds.), *Handbook of mixed methods in social and behavioral research* (pp. 3–50). Thousand Oaks, CA: Sage.

Teddlie, C., & Tashakkori, A. (2009). *Foundations of mixed methods research: Integrati and qualitative approaches in the social and behavioral sciences*. Thousand Oaks, CA: Sage.

Urribarri, F. (2002). Castoriadis: The radical imagination and the post-Lacanian unconscious. *Thesis Eleven, 71*, 40–51.

Vagle, M. D., & Hofsess, B. A. (2016). Entangling a post-reflexivity through post-intentional phenomenology. *Qualitative Inquiry, 22*(5), 334–344. https://doi.org/10.1177/1077800415615617

7 Integration using imagination processes and arts-based practices

In this chapter, the induction of imaginative mental processes and arts-based practices into strategies for conceptualization, investigation, and integration in research, and in particular mixed methods research, are explored from philosophical and methodological perspectives. Specifically, this exploration posits that these perspectives and practices might complement existing integration strategies in mixed methods research. The hallmark of mixed methods research, and indeed its most challenging aspect, is that of integrating diverse forms of qualitative and quantitative data that represent a pluralistic onto-epistemic resulting in holistic outcomes and insights. The challenges of encountering such a complex pluralistic onto-epistemology represented by diverse ideata/data, which is resistant to traditional unidimensional thought and method, presents opportunities to embrace and use multi-dimensional dynamic imaginative and creative approaches to analyzing, translating, and interpreting data. As affirmed by Greene (2007), the interaction and integration of data in mixed methods research "represents an opportunity for creative ideas and imaginative thinking" (p. 144). Imaginative mental processes and arts-based practices are particularly relevant to addressing the challenges and opportunities of integrating diverse forms of data/ideata in mixed methods approaches because this mode of thinking and knowing expects engagement with multi-dimensional ambiguous phenomena, multiple voices of participants, and the diverse forms of visible and invisible ideata/data at sensory, embodied, and imaginal levels. With the aims of exploring new relationships between diverse ideata/data, mining for multiple dimensions of knowledge, and increasing in-depth understanding, imagination allows us to reach beyond the tangible, visible, and logical to touch the other and re-imagine constructs otherwise entrenched and inaccessible from traditional research perspectives. A deeply creative and reflective process of engaging with ideata/data through introspective and intersubjective reverie, improvisational artistic inquiry, and dialectical dialogues embrace ambiguity and tension resulting in a rich synthesis of multiple perspectives, meaningful

DOI: 10.4324/9781003260189-7

insights, and illuminative discoveries about the phenomena under study (Abdullah, 2016; Archibald & Gerber, 2018; Camargo-Borges, 2018; Haiven & Khasnabish, 2014; Kapitan, 2010; Montuori, 2011).

To highlight parallels between imaginative processes, arts-based practices, and integration in mixed methods research, it may be helpful to introduce the investigative and interpretive parallel concept of translation in arts-based research. Translation "as we understand it, is a concept and practice that represents not only the transformation of one language into another, but more comprehensively the transformation of one form of knowledge into another" (Gerber & Myers-Coffman, 2018, p. 587). The process of translation in arts-based research includes intersectional and iterative processes of *formation, assemblage, construction, synthesis, interpretation, and representation* as sensory, embodied, emotional, and imaginal ideata emerge, take shape, transform, acquire coherency and meaning in language, symbols, visual art, and/or performance. The purpose of translation is to identify and transform the pre-verbal and pre-logical concepts and experiences, essential to the research and human phenomena, from unconscious to conscious constructs, from the unknown to the known, from the invisible to the visible, from meaningless to meaningful.

It could be proffered that these translational processes resemble those integration practices in mixed methods research in that they aim to embrace, synthesize, and transform multiple and diverse forms of not-yet-known knowledge. Therefore, the arts-based translational processes of *forming, assembling, constructing, interpretating, and synthesizing* might be conceptualized as aligned or juxtaposed with integrational mixed methods practices of *building, connecting, comparing, merging, and assimilating* to create a framework for the inclusion of imaginative processes and arts-based practices (Gerber & Myers-Coffman, 2018; Guetterman & Fetters, 2018; Pluye et al., 2018). It is important to note that these concepts and associated practices create a dynamic process rather than a prescriptive method to guide ways of thinking about, reflecting upon, and processing complex forms of ideata/data. Consequently, these processes are not formulaic or linear but rather dynamic meandering, iterative, improvisational, intersubjective, and constructivist, providing room for engaging with, responding to, uncovering, conceptualizing, identifying, living into, assembling, re-assembling, illuminating, integrating, representing, and assigning meaning to diverse forms of emergent data. The types and relevance of ideata/data that emerge during this process may not be immediately apparent but rather exist on the periphery of consciousness and in the in-between spaces and intersubjective crevices. Thus, beginning as a notion, a spontaneous image, a dream, a nagging feeling, a sensation, or an embodied response to questions, these ideata/data beg for recognition require nurturing and coaxing. The premise here is that these notions, images, emotions, and sensations, previously unknown and dismissed, do in fact have relevance to and offer insights into multiple phenomena and types of ideata/data requiring our considered attention. As Edwards et al. (2017) proffer, the exercise of assembling combining artistic and scientific practices within a single process employs necessary "deterritorializations and rhizomatic processes . . . [which are] sometimes called anti-method" (p. 182). This anti-method embraces pre-logical, rhizomatic thinking, and dialectic processes that are uncertain and uncomfortable "disrupt[ing] efforts to consolidate observations into a theoretical perspective so as to pursue new openings" (Edwards et al., 2017, p. 183).

Although it should be noted that the focus of this chapter is on the translational and integrative phase of mixed methods research, these imaginative arts-based strategies may need to be or can be employed during some or all phases of the research to further: conceptualize the dimensions of the research topics; to envision and re-envision methodological approaches; to visualize, attune to, reflect upon participants; to reflect upon the crevices and spaces in the generated ideata/data; to create and develop triangulation and integrative strategies; and to form, assemble, construct, interpret, and represent the ideata/data.

What follows is a theoretical proposal of how the translational concepts in imaginative and arts-based processes and practices might intersect with and inform the integration concepts and practices in mixed methods research. This proposal is in no way conclusive nor is each category meant to be distinct from one another or confined to a linear or phasic implementation; but rather it is presented as a dynamic way of engaging with iterative, innovative, and imaginative ways of approaching, thinking about, and exploring the multiple dimensions and concealed meaning in, between, and around the data.

Forming, building, and connecting

In arts-based research translation, forming is a process driven by the existential concept of *poiesis* or "creating something from nothing [and] . . . an avoidance of intentional coherence or representation through emergent, free associative random arts-based expressions" (Gerber & Myers-Coffman, 2018, p. 601). Forming resembles and mirrors how we encounter ideata/ data in the form of images, sensations, emotions in everyday life and, how they become a part of our perception, interpretation, and understanding of the world. But these ways of knowing are often beyond our consciousness while simultaneously and insidiously infiltrating our individual and collective unconscious or guiding frame of reference (Bollas, 2002; Swan-Foster, 2018). In research as in daily life, these illusive ideata/data hold clues to our perceptions, motivations, and behaviors. Therefore, in the formative phase of translation in arts-based research, the use of *free association, spontaneous artmaking and improvisation, reverie, improvisational intersubjective arts-based dialogues, and nonrepresentational imaginative and/or artistic responses* provide access to these pre-verbal aesthetic ideata/data disrupting the usual modes of thought, transcending the logical, exposing the concealed and invisible, and allowing for unexpected but welcome revelations. During this phase, the researcher may employ fluid, sensory, and emotive media in singular or multiple arts genres such as paints, pastels, or clay in the visual arts, due to their spontaneous evocative nature; and/or improvisational movement, free writing, musical improv and the like to elicit, gather and form these aesthetic ideata/data. The researcher engages in these imaginative and spontaneous arts practices both individually and through improvisational intersubjective dialogues to further elicit artifacts and authenticate socially constructed and ideata/data-driven perspectives. Thus, the forming process employs dynamic and iterative rhizomatic thinking, critical reflection, and free associative dialectical dialogues, to retrieve these liminal unconscious artifacts that live between qualitative and quantitative dichotomies, bring them into consciousness, and begin to sculpt, shape, and construct meaning.

As I write I entertain mental pictures of my words popping into my mind like a dream—emerging from nowhere. I want to catch them, capture them, pluck from them the unconscious and gently urge them into consciousness. Please do not disappear until I can draw you! These fleeting and beautiful images are begging for recognition and attention, float like a mobile aligning with other fragments of ideas, images and sensations. I can see and feel them, I want to touch them, and form or sculpt them. I attend to those images as my fingers type and try to translate those visualizations into another and incompatible medium of words. As I translate these illusive mental images into actual drawings, paintings, sculptures or collages the dialogue begins and their stories, intersections, relevance, and meaning are revealed. This is imagination in research!

Forming is not an end point but rather a beginning phase as well as an ongoing process, used iteratively as necessary to, explore intimate connections within the ideata/data – what lies in between and around the ideata/data, between researcher and researched (Gemignani, 2011; Gerber & Myers-Coffman, 2018; Springgay et al., 2008) "where meanings reside in the simultaneous use of language, images, materials, situations, space and time" (Springgay et al., 2008, p. 19). The forming process contributes to the disruption, deconstruction, and extraction of essential data otherwise obscured by logic and hidden within and between the text and statistical data. The emergence of these formative ideata/data and connections between them become the precursors to the revelation and construction of integrative meaning.

A comparable approach to the formative phases of translation in mixed methods research integration may be *building* or *connecting* in sequential studies when one form of data is used to form and inform the next phase of the research. For instance, in exploratory studies, qualitative textual, visual, or descriptive data are typically used to inform and form the development of a quantitative measure built upon qualitative thematic constructs; while in explanatory studies the qualitative in-depth descriptive investigation explores and builds upon the identified liminal data spaces in the quantitative data during the qualitative phase (Creswell & Plano Clark, 2011; Guetterman & Fetters, 2018). Connecting in mixed methods research references the critical, reflective, and systematic connection between quantitative or statistical results and textual, visual, and other thematic descriptive data drives the integrative meaning-making of the results (Pluye et al., 2018). Likewise, the process of transforming qualitative data into thematic constructs conducive to quantification or extraction of essential quantified variables for further exploration. Both of these connection processes are equally challenging, requiring imagination as well as critical analysis, credibility, and veracity (Greene, 2007).

It is proposed that imaginative processes and arts-based practices such as free *association, spontaneous mark-making, doodles, memos, poetry, movements, enactments, improvisational intersubjective dialogues*, which are more attuned with unconscious, pre-representational, sensory-embodied concepts, can find, reveal, and elicit previously illusive not-quite-formed fragments, notions, themes, and variables hiding in the in-between data spaces. Furthermore, such exploratory and elicitation processes create visualizations, alignments, and connections illuminating obscure data and their intersections. These formative processes lead to the related and next-step process of assemblage in translation or integration practices. During the assemblage process, the formative sensations, associations, and visualizations collected during the formative stage are assembled creating new integrative constructions.

Yikes! I have all of these ideata/data and I am completely stumped and stunned -- how do I understand these ideata/data and their relationship to one another? My mind is a blank and my anxiety is high. So, I decide to use the blankness and the anxiety to understand the ideata/data-- what about the ideata/data induces these responses or is it just my own performance anxiety? I take out my sketchpad and some random art materials--pencils, markers, crayons--I dive into the nothingness of the white paper mindful of the mantra of trusting the process. I make a mark, and add color, I let my mind wonder, wander, and converse with the fragmentary marks on the paper- -"trust the process I tell myself". An image starts to emerge, and I follow it. The image sparks other images and relationships between the images. A story starts to emerge. I know if I keep going it will open my mind to the ideata/data and insights into relationships and meaning.

Assemblage, comparing, and constructing

In arts-based translation, the researcher moves fluidly between immersive and incubative (Moustakas, 1990) processes during these dynamic and interactive phases of analysis and synthesis. Such is the case with forming and assemblage. The formative stage emphasizes reliance upon unconscious, spontaneous, and imaginative elicitations to mine for illusive data and connections. In assemblage or construction, the researcher more intentionally begins to imagine, arrange, connect, and re-construct the spontaneous pre-representational sense-based and embodied artifacts generated in the formative phases of the research into what will eventually become a coherent either textual or arts-based representation of the phenomena under investigation. The assemblage and construction process employs an imaginative and intentional exploration of the dialectical tensions between arts-based preverbal and pre-logical expressions and emergent logical textual, visual, or statistical data through arranging, juxta positioning, living in-between, re-arranging, pulling apart, and putting together the artifacts collected during the formative phases. This process disrupts the usual tendencies toward more linear and convergent alignments of the presenting data and emphasizes the typically unthought of or dismissed illogical, rhizomatic, and creative thinking.

Inherent in the assemblage process is moving from the individual researcher/ participant position to collaborative intersubjective reveries, arts-based dialogues, and constructions which include both diverse data and multiple voices.

Translating and interpreting the sense-and body-based narratives emergent from the formative stage and subsequent iterative constructions within the intersubjective context maintain the focus of ABR on investigating human relational phenomena, while maintaining the rigor, authenticity, credibility, and resonance in ABR.

(Gerber & Myers-Coffman, 2018, p. 603)

The intersubjective dialogic aspect of assemblage contributes to the gathering, forming, sculpting, and transforming of the fragments, artifacts, and ambiguous pre-representational knowledge into more socially constructed narratives, symbols, and metaphors. "The result of this collaboration is the co-construction of human narratives arising out of the sensory embodied data and finding intersubjective resonance and representation amongst the co-researchers" (Gerber & Myers-Coffman, 2018, p. 604).

Within the individual and intersubjective assemblage processes, various arts genres and art mediums may be used strategically to further in-depth mining of specific data or data spaces to extract, amplify, explore, and illuminate essential aspects of the research phenomena. For instance, in the visual arts during the formative stages, more fluid, sensory, and emotive media such as paints or pastels may be used due to their more spontaneous nature. While during assemblage and construction processes, more rigid and cognitive media such as collage, pencil illustration, or sculptural approaches may be used to construct and assemble the formative expressions into emerging symbolic and metaphoric representations. Some of these genres and approaches might be but are not limited to "developing" *poetry, collages, stories or vignettes, choreographies, concept maps, musical reflections and compositions, movement phrases, sculptural constructions, dramatic improvisations, and enactments*, using the dynamic interaction between individual and collaborative efforts. Additionally, storying statistics, writing narratives (Pluye et al., 2018), and/or engaging in imaginative variation (Moustakas, 1994) conducted both individually and collectively, evoke the emergence of new visualizations, conceptualizations, and ultimately construction of arts-based structures that amplify, integrate, and assign meaning to diverse data.

As referenced previously, these imaginative and arts-based assemblage processes include the evocation and emergence of symbolic representations of the phenomena. Symbols often "become the ultimate translational mechanism in that they can carry meaning from one form of knowledge to another while maintaining the aesthetic and emotional integrity" (Gerber &

Myers-Coffman, 2018, p. 604). Symbols are ideal integrative, compact carriers of our histories, narratives, and ideata/data in that multiple ideas, artifacts, and experiences can be condensed and concisely represented by an image, poem, or musical piece which convey a powerful message, initiate an aesthetic intersubjective dialogue, and evoke an emotional response from the audience relative to the phenomenon under study.

In this translational stage, the formative fragments of the pre-representational ideata/data are assembled and re-assembled, the relationships between them identified, and new insights emerge using multiple imaginative and arts-based practices, genres, and planes. Similar processes may occur as we evaluate the convergences and divergences of qualitative and quantitative data in mixed methods research. Arts-based translational processes of assembling, comparing, and constructing these diverse artifactual ideata/data are not unlike those processes of integration required when evaluating the intersections between qualitative and quantitative data. As Pluye et al. (2018) describe in their comparative integrative approach, the focus is on the dialectic tension between the similarities and differences wherein "discrepancies, contradiction, discordances, or dissonances" are decisively examined as a source of insight and knowledge (pp. 46–47).

Although seemingly similar thought processes, some might argue that there are major differences between translational and integration approaches in ABR and MMR. Typically, the types of data and the ways in which these data are conceptualized, arranged, juxtaposed, compared, and constructed seem to be, on-the-face, different in ABR and MMR. For instance, in mixed methods integration researchers typically are aligning textual and statistical data while in ABR, the focus is on the juxta positioning of more sensory, embodied, and imaginal emergent ideata/data. Therefore, MMR researchers may propose that the comparisons and integration of convergent divergent data occur on a singular linear plane relating one variable to one thematic correlate using one-dimensional tables, diagrams, and other comparable visual displays; while ABR researchers employ multiple dynamic spatial interactive imaginative processes and arts-based practices to explore the dimensions of the data and their relationship to each other. What if the MMR researchers were to consider shifting to the artist's mind referenced earlier – to disrupt the usual familiar scientific thinking of singularity and linearity and open to critically engaging with data on these spatial, dynamic, and interactive planes? Edwards et al. (2017) suggest that scientists need to dismiss structures or theories in order to discover and construct or assemble new knowledge. The imaginative arts-based translational approaches introduce rhizomatic thinking, multiple planes, and dimensions by which hidden data can be elicited from the in-between spaces for re-conceptualization, re-visualization, connections, alignment, and interpretation resulting in new perspectives and insights. Therefore, it is proposed these two approaches, dialectical dialogues between linear logical planes and spatial, multi-dimensional, intersubjective arts-based assemblages, allow for the exploration of the in-between spaces, the construction and assemblage of new data relationships, and the revelation of the underlying meanings in the research phenomena.

As I write this section, as usual, I see flashes of images in my mind of data climbing out of the dark spaces and crevices in between the numbers and the text, the creation of new ideas from the friction and tension between them almost like result of an earthquake-- the opening of a new crag in the earth, the ideas clawing their way into the light, the discoveries in a cave, shining a light in the dark, rubbing two ideas together and creating lightening and enlightenment. These new artifacts are discovered, arranged, rearranged, and then assembled--how do they relate to one another and what stories do they tell and what voices do they represent? How do I understand the data differently, more holistically, alive, dynamic, and meaningful?

Final synthesis and assimilation

> The final synthesis in the arts-based research translational process is when through intensive engagement in the previous formative, iterative, constructive, and intra and intersubjective dialogic translational processes, the cumulative data and associated insights become artfully reconfigured into either a final performance, installation, narrative, poetry anthology, or other form of arts-based representation.
>
> (Gerber & Myers-Coffman, 2018, p. 604)

The final synthesis in the arts-based translational process involves the transformation of the artifacts, constructions, and narratives that have emerged throughout the formative and assemblage phases into another art form or performance that represents the whole of the research. In other words, the final synthesis builds, connects, assimilates, and transforms the cumulative ideata/data from the previous formative and assemblage processes into a ideata/data-driven arts-based visual arts exhibit, installation, prosaic or poetic work, dramatic enactment, performance, or other arts genre. Essential in this creative final synthesis process is the use of metaphor and symbolism which act as synthesizers and interpreters representing the integrative result from the researchers' immersion in the previous imaginative and arts-based translational processes. "The results incorporate the metaphoric and symbolic representations of the cumulative and emergent arts-based data, the ultimate goal of which is to offer a coherent, aesthetically powerful, and intersubjectively resonant arts-based representation of the phenomena under investigation" (Gerber & Myers-Coffman, 2018, p. 604). Thus, the final synthesis seamlessly, concisely, critically, and authentically represents the research phenomena resulting in an evocative aesthetic outcome available to the audience. The final synthesis embraces the gathering, artful, and dialectical integration of multiple diverse ideata, data, and aesthetic experience. It is the result of careful, critical, and systematic consideration of all arts-based, aesthetic, and narrative ideata/data collected during the research in response to the research question. It is simultaneously the result of an emergent imaginative, creative, engaged, and embodied lived experience and interpretation of these ideata/data. The final synthesis represents the ultimate critical creative research process through honoring the tension between and the convergence of diverse forms of ideata/data through imagination, interpretation, and representation. The result of this creative synthesis is sort of a hybrid between systematic critical evaluation and a magical alchemy by which these elements come together to form an arts-based result carrying meaning, aesthetic power, and social impact.

Victoria Scotti (as cited in Gerber & Myers-Coffman, 2018) describes her final synthesis process following an intensive analysis of arts-based and narrative data from five women experiencing the transition to motherhood. In the final stages of her research, she had created both individual in-depth and group portraits of these women in response to the interview and artistic data collected from the participants. During the process of her arts-based exploration and portraiture, she became intimately acquainted with the data and the women they represented. As she moved toward creating the final synthesis, she had a sudden insight and inspiration (Scotti & Gerber, 2017).

During data analysis, it became apparent that I was working with the data and there were certain themes, clusters of themes that were in common. All the participants started kind of talking between themselves . . . so the dramatic form seemed to be well fitted for that kind of data.

(Scotti as cited in Gerber & Myers-Coffman, 2018, p. 604)

Evoked by the immersion in the arts-based and narrative data, the systematic and critical creative analysis of these data, the formation and assemblage of the results, and her own data-driven artistic process, the conceptualization of the final synthesis, seemingly spontaneous or alchemical, was perfectly aligned with, emergent from, and driven by the data. The authentic voices of these women, who she by then knew so well, began a discourse in her mind which she decided would best represent the essence of their lived experience as performed in a play. This epiphany or illumination is typical of the imaginative process, arts-based practice, and translation when systematically exploring a research phenomenon.

The closest approximation of these translational processes of final synthesis to integration in mixed methods research may be partially apparent in all proposed models, but perhaps are most aligned with those of merging (Creswell & Plano Clark, 2011) and assimilation (Pluye et al., 2018). In these strategies, one form of data is transformed into another for purposes of assessing the alignment, misalignment, and the tensions in-between diverse qualitative and quantitative data sets during final integration and meaning making. Similar to the interdependence of formative, assemblage, and synthesis translational processes in art-based practices, integrative approaches of merger or assimilation may indeed depend explicitly or implicitly on a cumulative synthesis of insights from related processes such as building, connection, and/or comparisons, all contributing to the transformation of the data.

Ultimately, in mixed methods research, the final assimilation or merger generally refers to the quantitative data being narrated or richly described; the thematic qualitative data becoming quantified or enumerated as variables; or the coherent construction of a case description including all qualitative and qualitative data (Pluye et al., 2018). The results of the integrative practices in mixed methods may take various forms. They may be presented in a textual description or discussion, a diagram, or a visual display portraying the relationships of the convergences and divergences of the data. The outcomes of mixed methods research may lead to the development of a measure and/or an intervention, a deeper understanding of human phenomena, and the relationship of measure to meaning that represents a holistic perspective of the phenomena under investigation. The question is, would the insertion of imaginative processes and arts-based practices into the integration of diverse data in mixed methods research be useful in revealing the implicit data hiding in the liminal crevices between the quantitative and qualitative data contributing to the comprehensiveness of the result?

Final syntheses and integrative outcomes are subject to various forms of evaluation to ascertain credibility, authenticity, trustworthiness, and validity/reliability depending upon the research traditions. In mixed methods research, the integrative strategies are guided by, rigidly adherent to, and compliant with the existing evaluative criteria and procedures of validity or trustworthiness inherent in their respective traditions of quantitative and qualitative research (Pluye et al., 2018). The authenticity, credibility, and trustworthiness of arts-based results, often presented in an arts-based form, cannot be evaluated using the same philosophical assumptions or constructs as with these dominant paradigms. Rather imaginative arts-based research ideata/data, content or results are most frequently judged by the audience engagement and witnessing of the final process/product. The aesthetic power and truthfulness, evocative impact, resonance, usefulness and relevance, concision, incisiveness and comprehensiveness, multiplicity, and simultaneity of meaning, have been cited as potential evaluative criteria (Barone & Eisner, 2012; Leavy, 2020). Gerber and Myers-Coffman (2018) posit that the "capacity to retain the pluralistic, ambiguous, non-temporal, and simultaneous aspects of arts-based knowledge through the construction of symbolic and metaphoric interpretations of the data conveys the meaning and preserves the authenticity through narratives and artistic representations" (p. 604). Thus, the evaluation of the credibility of arts-based research is typically determined by how it resonates with and impacts the intended audience; and, in some cases, if this emotional and evocative impact can disrupt the usual to raise questions about existing sociopolitical constructs (Gerber et al., 2020). The infusion of imaginative and arts-based practices into mixed methods research thus raises questions as to evaluative approaches and the necessity of reconsidering the worldviews or underlying assumptions about research and its credibility. Certainly, paradigms such as the dialectical stance (Greene, 2007) and dialectical pluralism (Johnson, 2015) allow for and applaud the inclusion and tensions between multiple worldviews within mixed methods research. So, if the imaginative and arts-based practices are included in mixed methods research, researchers will have to engage in creative critical reflections, innovative methods of evaluation, and perhaps shifts in thinking about assumptions regarding philosophy, theory, data, evidence, method, and credibility in research. Such shifts, as mentioned earlier, require the movement from objective/subjective binary thinking and methods of evaluation to a pluralistic dialectic intersubjective ontology and a partner epistemology inclusive of multiple interactive dynamic voices and forms of knowledge. Within such a paradigm, could the criteria such as aesthetic power, evocativeness, usefulness, relevance, and resonance be added to existing measures to evaluate the authenticity, credibility, and value of research that embraces mixed and arts-based practices (Barone & Eisner, 2012; Leavy, 2020)?

Summarily, the induction of imaginative processes and arts-based practices specific to the integration of diverse ideata/data in mixed methods research are described and illustrated in this section. These imaginative and arts-based translational processes of forming, assembling, constructing, interpreting, synthesizing, and representing can be viewed as parallel to a combination of mixed methods research integrative principles of building, comparing, connecting, merging, and assimilating. It is posited that there is a complementarity between these philosophies, processes, and practices which are dynamic, iterative, dialectic, and multi-dimensional; and that these processes and practices have the same goal of revealing, illuminating, synthesizing, and making meaning from pluralistic intersubjective realities and the resident eclectic and diverse ideata/data.

For purposes of review, the imaginative mental processes and arts-based practices include the forming or formative processes such as free association, evocative reveries, spontaneous formative arts processes, intersubjective improvisation; followed by assembling, merging, connecting and building processes of juxta positioning arranging, comparing, putting together, tearing apart, filling in the spaces, moving around using multiple arts mediums and genres; followed by interpretation and representation in the final synthesis and integration through intersubjective constructive arts-based dialogues, deconstructing and re-assembling, re-contextualizing, condensing and symbolizing, reassembling and final synthesis (Butler-Kisber & Poldma, 2010; Chilton & Scotti, 2014; Gerber & Myers-Coffman, 2018; Lawrence-Lightfoot, 2018; Manders & Chilton, 2013; Sajnani, 2013). Table 7.1 provides a succinct summary, synthesis, and guide for integrating imaginative processes and arts-based practices into various phases of research. Creative and illuminating solutions that embrace fresh outlooks, inclusive processes, and multiple approaches to conceptualization, research practice, and evaluative criteria for both integration and translational veracity may indeed open our collective minds to new insights and creative, radically imaginative world perspectives.

Table 7.1 Translational and integrative imaginative processes and arts-based practices

Imaginative Process	Definition	Arts-Based Practices	Phases of Research
Forming and Building Free Association	Engaging in evocative reveries allowing one's mind to wander eliciting formative sensory-embodied impressions and images (e.g., pre-logical sensory, visual, movement, sound, music, etc.)	1 Free associative mark, sound, and movement making 2 Spontaneous random arts-based responses, movements, music, etc. 3 Doodling	• Forming • Building 1 Conceptualization 2 Phenomena 3 Questions
Spontaneous Formative Art-Processes	Improvisational use of single or multiple arts-based genres	1 Spontaneous mark-making, movement, utterances, sounds, etc. 2 Free writing 3 Improvisational music, movement, enactments, poetry	• Forming • Building 1 Design 2 Procedures

Intersubjective Improvisational Dialogues	Interactive formative enactments of sensory, embodied, emotional and imaginal responses reflecting on research phenomena, diverse data, and attunement to participants	1 Responsive interactive movement, music, poetry, stories or visual images to spontaneous or free associative elicitations 2 Recording and documenting interactive arts-based dialogues and spontaneous utterances 3 Formative discussion and arts-based response	• Assemblage • Comparing • Connecting • Constructing	1 Clarification of questions and design 2 Participant attunement 3 Ethics 4 Data generation strategies
Intentional and Strategic Use of Art Media	Intentional and strategic use of artistic media to enhance, intensify, amplify, clarify, or synthesize. Transitioning from one phase to another through media change, exploring in more depth, or introducing another perspective	1 Intersubjective dialogues 2 Insertion of new medium (dance, music, drama poetry, visual art) 3 Narratives 4 Videos 5 Portrayals 6 Medium continuum – fluid-rigid 7 Moving from nonrepresentational random elicitations to representational coherent images, sounds, movements, etc.	• Forming and assembling • Comparing and connecting	1 Data generation strategies 2 Phases and strands 3 Qual and quan positioning 4 Data analysis/translation 5 Integration

(Continued)

Table 7.1 (Continued)

Imaginative Process	Definition	Arts-Based Practices	Phases of Research
Assemblage, Comparing, and Constructing			
Assembling	Juxtapositioning assembling of pre-logical sensory, visual, movement, sound, music, etc. with free associations, logical language, arranging, combining, tearing apart rearranging and filling in the spaces	1 Collages 2 Concept mapping 3 Visual portrayals 4 Narrations 5 Musical pieces 6 Dramatic Enactments 7 Poetry 8 Stories	• Assembling • Merging • Building • Connecting 1 Data generation 2 Data analysis 3 Translation 4 Integration
Re-assembling, Re-arranging, Deconstructing, Reconstructing	Reconceptualizing preliminary assemblages by taking them apart, rearranging them, and reconstructing as meaning begins to emerge	1 Collages 2 Metaphors 3 Concept mapping 4 Visual portrayals 5 Narrations 6 Musical pieces 7 Dramatic enactments 8 Poetry 9 Stories	• Assembling • Constructing • Merging • Connecting • Building 1 Data analysis 2 Translation 3 Integration

Recontextualization and Imaginative Variation	Imagining the data outside of its current context, in an unlikely context, and re-situating data in another place and narrative – in a new place	1 New scene 2 Collaging 3 Metaphors 4 Concept mapping 5 Context mapping 6 Storying and re-narrating	• Assembling • Constructing • Synthesizing • Merging • Connecting • Building	1 Data analysis 2 Translation 3 Integration
Intersubjective Constructive Arts-Based Dialogues	Relational reflection, formation, sculpting, and transforming the individual fragments and ambiguous pre-representational data into socially constructed assemblages	1 Collages 2 Metaphors 3 Vignettes 4 Choreographies 5 Musical reflections 6 Movement phrases 7 Dramatic enactments 8 Storying statistics 9 Writing narratives	• Assembling • Constructing • Synthesizing • Merging • Connecting • Building	1 Data analysis 2 Translation 3 Integration

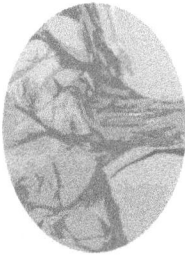

(Continued)

Table 7.1 (Continued)

Imaginative Process	Definition	Arts-Based Practices	Phases of Research
Final Synthesis			
Condensation and Symbolization	Re-assembling, putting together, and filling in the spaces Identifying emergent symbols and metaphors that authentically represent the ideata/data and are responsive to the research phenomena	1 Putting together 2 Combining 3 Filling in the empty spaces 4 Dynamic spontaneity and intentionality 5 Portraying 6 Storying 7 Metaphor and symbol formation	• Translation • Merging • Connecting • Building • Synthesis 1 Data analysis 2 Translation 3 Integration
Synthesis	Final assemblage and synthesis of the ideata/data Constructing a coherent image(s), story, play, dance, composition, poem, installation that is ideata/data driven and aesthetically powerful	1 Putting together 2 Collaging/concept mapping 3 Imaginative variation 4 Storying 5 Symbolization 6 Textual descriptions 7 Arts-based representations 8 Exhibit/performance 9 Audience feedback	• Translation • Merging • Connecting • Building • Synthesis 1 Integration 2 Interpretation 3 Final synthesis

Source: All images original creations by Nancy Gerber

References

Abdullah, M. T. (2016). *Metaphorical imagination: Towards a methodology of implicit evidence*. Cambridge Scholars Publishers.

Archibald, M., & Gerber, N. (2018). Arts and mixed methods research: An innovative methodological merger [Special issue]. *American Behavioral Scientist*. Advance online publication. https://doi.org/10.1177/0002764218772672

Barone, T., & Eisner, E. (2012). *Arts based research*. Sage Publications Inc.

Bollas, C. (2002). *Free Association*. Icon Books.

Butler-Kisber, L., & Poldma, T. (2010). The poser of visual approaches in qualitative inquiry: The use of collage making and concept mapping in experiential research. *Journal of Research Practice*, *6*(2). Retrieved November 8, 2019 from http://jrp.icaap.org/index.php/jrp/article/view/197/196

Camargo-Borges, C. (2018). Creativity and imagination: Research as worldmaking. In P. Leavy (Ed.), *Handbook of arts-based research* (pp. 88–100). Guilford Press.

Chilton, G., & Scotti, V. (2014). Snipping, gluing and writing: The properties of collage as an arts-based research practice in art therapy. *Art Therapy: Journal of the American Art Therapy Association*, *31*(4), 163–171.

Creswell, J. W., & Plano Clark, V. L. (2011). *Designing and conducting mixed methods research* (2nd ed.). Sage Publications Inc.

Edwards, G., Arfaoui, A., McLaren, C., & McKeever, P. (2017). Hybrid health research: Assembling an integrated arts/science methodological framework. *Journal of Applied Arts & Health*, *8*(2). https://doi.org/10.1386/jaah.8.2.175_1

Gemignani, M. (2011). Between researcher and researched: An introduction to countertransference in qualitative inquiry. *Qualitative Inquiry*, *17*(8), 701–708. https://doi.org/10.1177/1077800411415501

Gerber, N., Biffi, E., Biondo, J., Gemignani, M., Hannes, K., & Siegesmund, R. (2020). Arts-based research in the social and health sciences: Pushing for change with an interdisciplinary global arts-based research initiative [35 paragraphs]. *Forum Qualitative Sozialforschung/Forum: Qualitative Social Research*, *21*(2). http://doi.org/10.17169/fqs-21.2.3496

Gerber, N., & Myers-Coffman, K. (2018). Translation in arts-based research. In P. Leavy (Ed.), *Handbook of arts-based research* (pp. 587–607). Guilford Press.

Greene, J. C. (2007). *Mixed methods in social inquiry*. Jossey-Bass Press.

Guetterman, T., & Fetters, M. (2018). Two methodological approaches to the integration of mixed methods and case study design: A systematic review. *American Behavioral Scientist*, *62*(7), 900–918.

Haiven, M., & Khasnabish, A. (2014). *The radical imagination: Social movement research in the age of austerity*. Zed Books Ltd.

Johnson, R. B. (2015). Dialectical pluralism: A metaparadigm whose time has come. *Journal of Mixed Methods Research*, *11*(2), 156–173. https://doi.org/10.1177/1558689815607692

Kapitan, L. (2010). *Introduction to art therapy research*. Routledge.

Lawrence-Lightfoot, S. (2018). *The art and science of portraiture*. www.saralawrencelightfoot.com/portraiture.html

Leavy, P. (2020). *Method meets art: Arts-based research practice* (2nd ed.). The Guilford Press.

Manders, E., & Chilton, G. (2013). Translating the essence of dance: Rendering meaning in artistic inquiry of the creative arts therapies. *International Journal of Education & the Arts, 14*(16), 1–17.

Montuori, A. (2011). Beyond postnomral times: The future of creativity and the creativity of the future. *Futures, 43*, 221–227.

Moustakas, C. (1990). *Heuristic research: Design, methodology and application.* Sage Publications Inc.

Moustakas, C. (1994). *Phenomenological research methods.* Sage Publications Inc.

Pluye, P., Bengoechea, E. G., Granikov, V., Kaur, N., & Tang, D. L. (2018). A world of possibilities in mixed methods: Review of the combinations of strategies used to integrate qualitative and quantitative phases, results and data. *International Journal of Multiple Research Approaches, 10*(1), 41–56.

Sajnani, N. (2013). Improvisation and art-based research. In S. McNiff (Ed.), *Art as research: Opportunities and challenges* (pp. 79–85). Intellect Ltd.

Scotti, V., & Gerber, N. (2017). Rendering *beyond words* in transitioning to motherhood through visual and dramatic arts. *Voices: A World Forum for Music Therapy, 17*(3), 1–17. https://doi.org/10.15845/voices.v17i3.924

Springgay, S., Irwin, R. L., Leggo, C., & Gouzouasis, P. (Eds.). (2008). *Being with a/r/tography.* Sense Publications.

Swan-Foster, N. (2018). *Jungian art therapy: A guide to dreams, images and analytical psychology.* Routledge.

8 Conclusion

In this book, we have explored the origins and nature of imagination and imagery in order to develop an understanding of the onto-epistemology and worldview that drive the integration of imaginative mental processes and arts-based practices in research. Furthermore, we introduced the concept that imaginative processes are essential to arts-based practices when used to enhance the depth of investigation for purposes of increased integration, insight, empathy, and illumination into complex human phenomena. Imagination was also discussed as both a meta-perspective and a micro-process. As a meta-perspective, we can examine the tacit knowledge structures of the sociopolitical culture and dominant research paradigms that unconsciously and perhaps insidiously guide our everyday thinking and our research decisions while simultaneously oppressing or obfuscating eclectic forms of knowledge and diverse or marginalized voices. As a micro-process, the infusion of imagination in research can introduce new philosophical assumptions, theories, and practices that can challenge the dominant sociopolitical and research paradigms, enable conscious and critical research decision making, increase the valuation of marginalized voices and forms of knowledge, disrupt the restrictive research traditions and thinking, and contribute to the enhancement of social discourse and accessibility of innovative research. Ideally, intersubjective and inclusive imaginative meta-perspectives and micro-processes can work in concert to create socially responsible and impactful research for change. It is proposed that essential and integral to full engagement in imaginative mental processes in research is the simultaneous implementation of arts-based investigative practices. The range of arts-based practices in research exist along a continuum from arts-related, arts-informed, and arts-based approaches. In this book, we advocated for embracing a strategic use of imaginative process and arts-based practices at various phases of the investigation to elucidate questions, reveal hidden ideata/data, and integrate results. Using imagination and the arts in research allows for the capacity to include unconscious

DOI: 10.4324/9781003260189-8

sensory-embodied ways of knowing, explore multiple ambiguous and paradoxical dimensions of knowledge, integrate diverse perspectives and voices, and reach beyond the obvious and the known into the realm of the unknown, concealed, or soon-to-be-known. The knowledge gained through these imaginative perspectives and arts-based practices allow us to touch, understand, and illuminate individual and collective human perceptions, motivations, and behaviors, otherwise inaccessible and concealed by traditional data and methods.

We have suggested that the dialectical aesthetic intersubjective onto-epistemic of imaginative processes and arts-based practices align particularly well with ways of viewing, understanding, and integrating the diverse forms of knowledge, particularly relevant in mixed methods research. In reviewing the integrative strategies for mixed methods research and the translational processes for imaginative arts-based research practice, we propose that the inclusion of arts-based investigative practices might contribute to a more authentic, in-depth, and comprehensive strategy for exploring the relationships between diverse and interactive qualitative and quantitative data – filling in the spaces that cannot be filled through traditional thinking, reasoning, or methods. Although mixed methods research adheres to traditional methods of evaluation based on qualitative and quantitative traditions, arts-based research evaluation criteria is reliant upon impact and feedback from the research audience. Including imaginative processes and arts-based practices into integrative research approaches provides an opportunity to expand perspectives and introduce critical and creative methods by which to view, understand, synthesize, and evaluate the measure, meaning, and resonance of multi-dimensional research.

Index

Note: Page numbers in **bold** indicate a table on the corresponding page.

For Product Safety Concerns and Information please contact our EU
representative GPSR@taylorandfrancis.com
Taylor & Francis Verlag GmbH, Kaufingerstraße 24, 80331 München, Germany